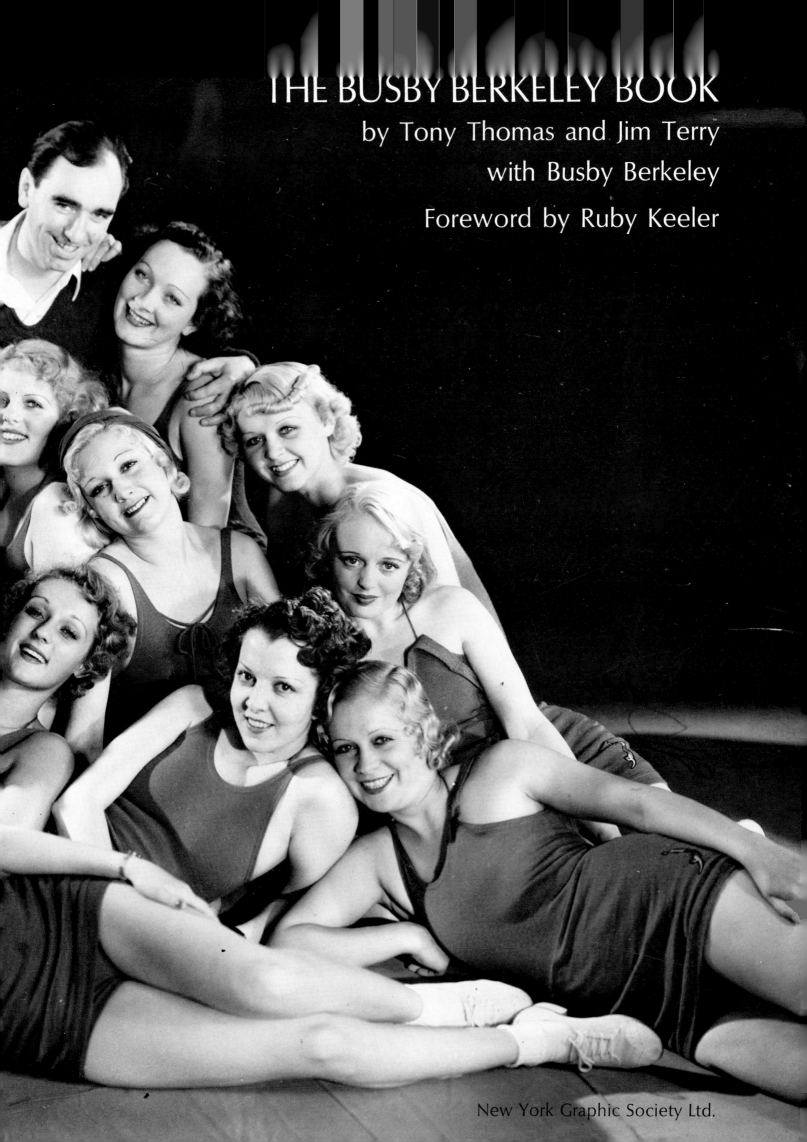

THE BUSBY BERKELEY BOOK

by Tony Thomas and Jim Terry

with Busby Berkeley

Foreword by Ruby Keeler

New York Graphic Society Ltd.

International Standard Book Number 0-8212-0514-5
Library of Congress Catalog Card Number 72-92874

Copyright © 1973 by Busby Berkeley and Jim Terry
All rights reserved. No portion of this book may be
reproduced or used in any form or by any means without
written permission of the publishers.
First published 1973 by New York Graphic Society Ltd.
140 Greenwich Ave., Greenwich, Conn. 06830
First printing 1973

Edited by Jane Salzfass
Designed by Don Sheldon and Marshall Berland

Manufactured in the U.S.A.

Dedicated
to my wife Etta,
whose boundless love and devotion
have been the inspiration
for this book

Busby Berkeley

Photograph Credits

Academy of Motion Picture Arts and Sciences, Library, Hollywood, Calif., 64
Audio-Visual Service, Los Angeles Public Library, 38
Paul Ballard, 157
Alan Barbour, 55 (top), 60, 62-63, 75, 84 (top), 86 (bottom), 102 (top)
Etta and Busby Berkeley, 10, 14, 15, 17, 18, 24, 28, 33, 65, 84, 86, 89 (bottom),
    94, 97, 100, 101, 102, 105, 106, 110, 116, 117 (top), 123, 125, 126, 128, 130,
    131, 133, 143, 144, 145, 146 (top), 147, 168-169, 174, 177, 181
Clarence Bull, 135 (bottom)
Cinemabilia, New York, 123, 135 (top)
Culver Pictures, 185
Jack Haley, 54, 90, 106 (sequence)
Loew's, Inc., 176, 178
Bert Longworth, Warner Bros., 25, 50 (top), 52, 56, 92
Memory Shop, New York, 34, 51 (right), 87
MGM Studios, 142, 182
Movie Star News, New York, 58 (center), 59, 88, 117 (center, bottom),
    146 (center, bottom)
The Museum of Modern Art/Film Stills Archive, New York, 44, 46, 51 (left),
    55 (bottom), 65 (right), 70-71, 74 (right), 82, 95, 99 (right), 114, 115, 121, 122,
    136-137, 142 (left), 159 (top right), 162, 166, 171, 177 (bottom)
Penguin Photo, New York, 53, 151, 152, 170 (top, bottom)
Erika Rabau, Berlin, 32
RKO Radio Pictures, Inc., 167
Springer/Bettman Film Archive, New York, 2-3, 103
Warner Brothers, 73, 118
Wide World Photos, 26, 27, 29, 30, 186, 189

Contents

Acknowledgments

The editors wish to thank the following people for their gracious assistance throughout the preparation of this book: Jim Baker, Alan Barbour, Robert Bonnard, Ernest Burns of Cinemabilia, Mary Corliss of the Film Stills Archive— The Museum of Modern Art, New York, Robert Essman, Ena Fielden of Penguin Studios, Ellen Forstenzer for mechanical preparation, Cheryl Clarke Gelley, Lloyd Harkema, Russ Jones, Linda Landis, Judy Litchfield, Ken Livesay, Bill O'Malley, Peggy O'Neill, Alice Parker, Steven Ross and Dorothy Swerdlove of the Theatre Collection Museum and Library of the Performing Arts at Lincoln Center, Wini Shaw, Ellie van Staagen.

We are deeply indebted to Mrs. Etta Berkeley for her unstinting enthusiasm and for placing so much valuable material from her private collection at our disposal.

"In an era of breadlines,
Depression and wars,
I tried to help people get away
from all the misery...
to turn their minds to something else.
I wanted to make people happy,
if only for an hour."

Berkeley directs Ruby Keeler in a scene from *Dames* (1934).

Foreword

"Just think, Ruby, this morning you were on a bus with nothing but a pair of tap shoes in your suitcase and a prayer in your heart. And now, you're not only a big Broadway star—the toast of Manhattan—you're the Sweetheart of the U.S. Navy. How does it feel?" asks Dick, the handsome sailor whose songs have just helped make the opening night of a Broadway show a smash hit. Lovely, young, innocent, talented Ruby from Centerville, U.S.A., replies, "Nice."

All right, fans. In what Hollywood musical did that scene originate?

Answer: In no Hollywood musical at all, but in a 1968 off-Broadway stage production that was a loving spoof of the movie musicals we made at Warner's in the 1930's, usually with songs by Al Dubin and Harry Warren and often starring Dick Powell, Joan Blondell, and yours truly. The authors had fashioned an amiable lampoon and done it with obvious affection and much good humor.

I know, and perhaps you know too, that such a show was a direct tribute to Busby Berkeley, and that without Busby Berkeley the good old Hollywood musical would have been much less than it was. In fact, it is almost entirely because of what he did that these pictures are still items of wonder and still amazing pieces of entertainment.

I met Buzz for the first time when I was brought from New York to Hollywood in 1932 to appear in *42nd Street*. Buzz had a reputation as a man who created fantastic musical numbers on Broadway and had already made a few movies. But it was what he did in *42nd Street* that made his name. Until then movie musicals had not been particularly impressive. The advent of sound had touched off a deluge of celluloid musicals, but the public quickly tired of seeing photographed singing and dancing. Producer Darryl F. Zanuck had to talk Warner's into doing *42nd Street;* he believed that a lavishly made musical with the best talent and proper presentation would bring the public to the box office in droves. What he needed was a brilliantly imaginative man to create and stage the musical numbers. Busby Berkeley was that man.

It was a fabulous era. Buzz created a wonderful world of his own, full of photographic trickery and hordes of pretty girls performing amazing routines. He was wild and daring and made his own rules, and in doing so he made music. All through the 1930's he dominated Warner Brothers' musical world with his fanciful geometric patterns, his bizarre montages of camera angles, his famous overhead shots, his kaleidoscopic effects, his cascades of designs—in short, with his highly cinematic imagination.

At its best the movie musical was a piece of fantasy, amusing because it was mostly an adventure in a never-never land. It was pure divertimento—unreal, improbable, escapist, pleasant, harmless hokum. No one watching a Busby Berkeley routine for a backstage musical like *Footlight Parade* bothered to concern himself with the fact that the routine was so gargantuan in scope it could never be contained on any theatre stage in the world. It simply didn't matter. It was meant only to be enjoyed.

More recently, I've had occasion to see these musicals again at festivals and tributes to Buzz at which I've been asked to appear. I'm always delighted to take part in any tribute to him because he truly deserves every round of applause. Hollywood is notorious for putting its pioneers out to pasture. Many years drifted by before it occurred to anyone that Busby Berkeley was the most distinctive cinematic-choreographic artist we have ever had in Hollywood.

Looking through the pages of this book brings back a great many memories for me. We have all forgotten so much! But now I recall the many times I stood on a sound stage and marveled at what Buzz did. He was a forceful, positive man bursting with ideas. He was into everything and seemed to know everything. He would argue with cameramen and composers and producers who would tell him that what he wanted couldn't be done. But it would be done, and done exactly as he wanted it. His attitude was that anything is possible. He was energetic, tireless, tough, and sometimes rough, but look at his pictures and tell me how any other kind of man could have achieved what he did.

The movie musical isn't what it was, but then, neither are most things. History has moved very fast these past few decades, and sitting in the dark watching *The Gold Diggers of 1933*, one could call it *The Gold Diggers of 1833* for all the relevance it has to today. Perhaps that's why it appeals to young people now, perhaps they see a life style light years removed from their own, perhaps they see an innocence long lost. Of course, what they also see are hundreds of tap dancers beating out "The Lullaby of Broadway," waltzing grand pianos, gorgeous girls marching in fantastic formations or sliding by dozens into waterfalls. You don't have to be young to be knocked out by all that.

No, they don't make movies like that any more. But the door to the sound stage is never completely shut, and the gauntlet lies outside waiting to be picked up. All it would take to make a film musical now would be a great story, filled with scintillating songs and dances performed by fascinating people and directed by a genius. I know such a man. His name is Busby Berkeley.

Ruby Keeler

New York
January 1973

THE MAN
BEHIND
THE SPECTACLE

Beginnings

BUSBY BERKELEY. The name stands alone as the creator of an entire genre of musical comedy films—among the very few directors whose work is unmistakable, indelible, unequaled. He is possibly more famous today than when *The Gang's All Here* was first shown thirty years ago. His achievement, his vision, was so unique that it is beyond time, beyond taste . . . with an extravagance and pure joy that remains fresh and unaffected today. This special Berkeley signature earned him a permanent place in film history. Truly larger than life, he created a unique realization of music on film, using only one camera to bring into being fantasies that will never be equaled. His genius is truly cinematographic—he uses film to do things that cannot be done in any other medium.

Berkeley's life has been like one of his films. He came from a theatrical family and there was the smell of greasepaint long before the roar of the crowd—the tough struggle to the top . . . the disastrous slide down, with a manslaughter trial after a tragic accident . . . the valiant climb back, mentally as well as professionally. And in classic Berkeley fashion, the final triumph—the recognition, awards, and standing ovations with an entire new generation of fascinated young people discovering films made before they were born.

Perhaps to make films that are remembered and revived is to achieve immortality. Certainly Berkeley has written a chapter in the history of that unique American film institution—the musical comedy.

Busby Berkeley was born November 29, 1895, in the proverbial theatrical trunk in Los Angeles. His parents were members of the Tim Frawley Repertory Company. His father, Francis Enos, was director of the company and an occasional actor; his mother, whose professional name was Gertrude Berkeley, was a character actress. They named their child Busby Berkeley William Enos, after two friends in the Frawley company, Amy Busby and William Gillette. Amy Busby was a young English soubrette who later became prominent on the London stage. William Gillette went on to become a star on Broadway as Sherlock Holmes in a play that he had written. Busby had a brother, George, ten years older. When Busby entered—stage left—George was away at military school. His parents toured the circuit with infant Busby in tow. Berkeley recalls, "My earliest memories go back to the age of five when my parents were playing Kansas City. I had a nurse, Annie, who was told to keep me away from the theatre at all times, except for the Saturday matinees. My parents' life in the theatre wasn't easy, and they wanted to keep me out of it. In those days, stock companies did a different play each week, with a performance every night, plus four matinees. They would do a drama one week, while rehearsing a comedy for the next week. They wanted to spare me that kind of life."

Gertrude Berkeley in stage costume.

Francis Enos, father of Busby Berkeley.

The New York Years

Busby's Debut

The Enoses tried to keep their oldest son, George, from going into the theatre as well. He graduated from Culver Military Academy, where he was an outstanding athlete and captain of the famous Culver Black Horse Troop. Nevertheless, it wasn't long before he broke down his parents' unwillingness and persuaded them to let him join their stock company. Young Busby was still denied entrance to the theatre, but managed to make his first stage appearance with George's help. "I had sneaked away from Annie and managed to slip by the stage doorman. I stood in the wings goggle-eyed, as the company played the Arabian desert drama *Under Two Flags*. George was one of the Arabs. He spotted me, and on his next entrance shoved me under his robe and walked onstage. There I stood, hidden from the audience, holding my brother's leg, scared stiff. That was my debut."

Gertrude Berkeley was popular in Missouri; she played Kansas City several years running and set up her own company, The Gertrude Berkeley Playhouse. But the strain of running the company and at the same time being its principal player brought on a nervous breakdown. This would be the first in a series of Enos family calamities.

After Gertrude regained her health, she and her husband were offered positions with a stock company in Washington, D.C., while George joined another company. As time went on, he drifted from place to place and his family heard from him only when he needed money.

While the Enoses were working in Washington, Busby's father was stricken with inflammatory rheumatism and was hospitalized. Gertrude, now the only breadwinner, accepted an offer to join the Castle Square Company in Boston, the finest stock company in America at that time.

Life Imitates Art

Busby, then eight years old, went to the theatre at night with his mother. "One of her roles turned out to be horribly ironic. She played a woman who had just lost her husband. In the first scene, she entered from the funeral, all in black. On opening night, just before she went on, we received a telegram that my father had died in the hospital in Washington. Steeling herself, my mother held back the tears and went on to play her part, not mentioning her own tragedy until the performance was over. This was the way I learned the principle that 'the show must go on.' "

The next few years were not easy for Gertrude and Busby. She took work where she could find it and often had to travel with touring stock companies.

NAZIMOVA IN "WAR BRIDES"

PATHETIC MOTHER ROLE MAKES NEW STAR FOR SCREEN

Gertrude Berkeley's Role In 'War Brides' Reveals Great Power to Make Audiences Weep.

Herbert Brenon's powerful photo-drama presentation of Nazimova in 'War Brides," the second Selznick-Picture, is in its second week of tremendous business at the Broadway Theatre. Since its gala opening this important Selznick-Picture has become the sensation of the motion picture world and appealed to two immense audiences each day.

The work of Gertrude Berkeley, as the mother of Joan in "War Brides," introduces a new and distinctive artist to the screen. Both Miss Berkeley and Nazimova play their difficult and pathetic roles so vividly that no titles or captions are really

Gertrude Berkeley and Nazimova in *War Brides*, the second Selznick silent film.

Busby was with her as much as possible and went to boarding schools and summer camps during the tours. A sensitive child, the boy became increasingly attached to his mother, with a growing respect for her devotion and indomitable spirit in keeping them both alive. In time the situation would reverse itself. Until her death at eighty-five, Gertrude continued to be the strongest influence on Berkeley—he in turn was an attentive and generous son.

Nazimova

At the age of twelve, Busby was enrolled in the Mohegan Lake Military Academy, near Peekskill, New York. He remained there for five years, visiting his mother on tour during holidays. As a respected character actress, Gertrude Berkeley had a certain fame. She came under the influence of the great Alla Nazimova, with whom she was associated for seven years, mostly doing Ibsen. Busby Berkeley's second stage appearance took place in Boston while his mother was playing with Nazimova in Ibsen's *A Doll's House.* "I was standing in the wings in my cadet uniform when Nazimova came by. She had with her two girls who were supposed to be her daughters. She took me by the hand and led me on-stage with the girls. It was a family scene and the audience thought I was just another one of the family. Afterwards, Nazimova congratulated me on my composure and told my mother I was a natural actor."

However, another tragedy loomed. George had not found himself as an actor and turned to drugs. His mother finally found out about his addiction to morphine and placed him in a sanitarium. He ran away several times, each time the addiction becoming more and more damaging to his health and spirit. One evening, during an engagement in New York, Gertrude received a telegram that her son had been found dead on a park bench in Plattsburgh, New York. The tragedy reinforced Busby's resolution to someday make his mother's life free from care.

Busby Berkeley was only average in scholastic studies at the Mohegan Military Academy, but excellent in sports, particularly football and baseball. However, Berkeley recalls, "I guess I had a little of the devil in me. I remember hanging alarm clocks down the hot-air registers in the assembly hall, timed to go off in the middle of the night. I also had a friend who owned a motorcycle and several times we climbed out of our windows on sheets tied together and whizzed into Peekskill to see what was going on. I never got caught doing that, but I got nailed for lots of other pranks."

Shoe Business

Busby Berkeley graduated from Mohegan Lake Military Academy in 1914. A school friend's father offered him an apprenticeship in his shoe company in Athol, Massachusetts. The offer was attractive, with the promise of a managing position once Busby learned the business. Always bright and eager, Busby accepted and enjoyed three years in Athol, advancing quickly in the business. The restless Berkeley also played semi-pro baseball, organized a dance band, and played in local shows.

Busby Berkeley, age 12, while attending Mohegan Lake Military Academy, New York.

"I can remember one occasion vividly. I was asked by the Women's Club of Athol to perform in a benefit for a local charity. I decided to recite 'The Soul of the Violin,' accompanied by an organ. It was a heart-rending piece about a destitute old fiddler who pawns his beloved violin to ward off starvation. He visits the violin now and then and talks to it, and each time he does so, a string breaks. When the last string breaks, the poor old man crumples to the floor and dies. I played it to the hilt. I had arranged for a friend of mine to stand by the light switchboard and cue the electrician to kill the lights when I dropped to the floor. Everything was going fine, the place was packed, mostly with church people, but as I got near my big finale, the lights suddenly went out and I was left in the dark. I yelled to the electrician, 'No, god-damn it, I'm not finished yet.' The audience howled. The lights came back on and I started to die all over again. I learned a lot about show business that night."

Uncle Sam Wants You

America's entry into the First World War changed the course of Busby Berkeley's life. With his military school training, and eager for adventure, he enlisted in the U.S. Army at Fort Banks, Massachusetts. He chose the artillery because he had heard they would be the first units sent to France. Berkeley requested officer's training and out of several hundred men in his battery, he was one of two chosen to be sent to Fort Oglethorpe, Georgia.

The spirit of mischief came back to mark his record as a trainee. "I got tired of the routine drills and told them I was an accomplished bugler. This was some-thing of an exaggeration, to say the least, but I got the job. One evening, just before taps, the boys were get-ting undressed when someone turned out the lights, and the place erupted into a whale of a pillow and water fight. I realized it was time for taps, so I reached for my bugle, but they shoved me out the door before I could get my clothes on. I stood there in the street, blowing taps stark naked. As I finished, I neatly about-faced. There stood the officer of the day! I lost my job as a bugler and consoled myself in the guardhouse."

Despite his pranks, Busby Berkeley was one of ninety-two men out of two thousand at Oglethorpe ordered to the famous Saumur Artillery School in France for special training. Berkeley recalls that the food on the crossing was miserable, but that he and a friend bribed a purser and spent the week on a diet of sourdough bread, Camembert cheese, and cham-pagne!

After landing, Berkeley and his companions hiked four miles to a camp on a hill overlooking Bordeaux, which was off-limits to them, but notorious for an underground red-light district, strictly patrolled by military police. Never one to be held back, Berkeley and a friend went AWOL, asking some pals to grunt their names when the roll was called. "We ended up at a little café, full of prostitutes. We both wanted to see the notorious Apache district and I asked one of the girls to get us some of their extra clothes. Then, dressed as girls and accompanied by a couple of tarts, we went into town. Underground Bordeaux was liter-ally that—two stories below street level, full of dark corridors leading to cellar cafés. The people were marvelous—when the M.P.'s raided the place, they hid us in packing cases. After two days and nights, we sneaked back into camp with no one the wiser."

The ninety-two artillery officer trainees finally ar-rived at Saumur and began instruction under French officers on the use of 75mm and 15mm howitzers. After three months, Berkeley received his commis-sion as a second lieutenant in the 312th Field Artillery of the 79th Division. The 312th was composed of six batteries of two hundred men each, and Berkeley was put in command of Battery F, to teach the men about French howitzers.

Lieutenant Busby Berkeley Enos

His First "Production Number"

Here in France, Busby Berkeley discovered the talent that would, years later, make him famous. Part of his duties was to conduct the parade drill. "I got tired of the old routine, and to make things more in-teresting, I asked the Colonel to let me try something different. I had worked out a trick drill for the twelve hundred men. I explained the movements by num-bers and gave the section leaders instructions for their companies and had them do the whole thing without any audible orders. Since the routines were numbered the men could count out their measures once they had learned them. It was quite something to see a parade square full of squads and companies of men marching in patterns, in total silence. The French Army asked if I would do the same for them, but our people refused permission."

Thus far, Berkeley had trained others, but was yet to see any action at the front. Hearing that the Army Air Corps needed volunteers, he applied for a transfer and landed in yet another training course—as an aerial observer. Soon after, the Armistice was signed; with no prospect of seeing action, Berkeley thought he would be happier if he went back to his old regiment. Signing a "refusal to fly," he was re-transferred.

The problem was now how to kill time in Europe. The Allies had troops in active service for years after the war, and keeping the men occupied proved more difficult than keeping the countries occupied. Entertaining servicemen now became a major enterprise, and one of Berkeley's first jobs on rejoining his regiment was to turn an old barn into a theatre. The YMCA sent out touring groups of entertainers (the USO had not yet been formed), and Berkeley contacted them to put on shows for his regiment.

Berkeley's regiment was shunted from place to place for no apparent reason, which did nothing for morale. Berkeley went AWOL—something that could have brought him a court-martial. "I wasn't deserting. I just took it into my mind to go absent without leave for a while. Late one night, I packed my duffel bag and went down to the station to wait for a train—any train, going anywhere. After a long wait, a freight train pulled in, and when it stopped to take on water, I sneaked into an empty boxcar. I sat crouched in a corner as we rode through the night. In the morning we arrived at Chaumont, General John J. Pershing's headquarters. In my weary mind I fully expected to be met by a firing squad, but no one even knew I was missing."

Berkeley collected his thoughts. He knew that Chaumont was the center for the YMCA's entertainment programming, run by Dorothy Donnelly, a well-known New York actress. Berkeley had an interview with Miss Donnelly and explained he wanted to be a director for the shows being sent out to the troops. She didn't seem particularly interested, until he mentioned he was Gertrude Berkeley's son. "She threw her arms around me and said, 'How wonderful! You're just the one I'm looking for. How would you like to be Entertainment Officer here in Chaumont?' I told her I would indeed, and within an hour or two, I was." Entertainment Officer Berkeley's joy was short-lived. An order had been issued for his arrest, and he was placed in the guardhouse at Chaumont. In the meantime, Dorothy Donnelly, with her considerable influence, had gone to General Pershing's office and persuaded his adjutant that Berkeley was badly needed in the entertainment forces and should be transferred from his regiment. The orders for his arrest were countermanded, and he was posted to Coblenz, Germany, as Assistant Entertainment Officer with the U.S. 3rd Army of Occupation.

Luck had so far played a great part in Busby Berkeley's life in the army and continued to do so. His superior officer in Coblenz was a Marine Corps Major named Steiner, who admitted that he knew nothing about show business and couldn't understand why he had been given the assignment. "Steiner was a good fellow. He took me to the officers' mess and over drinks said he would turn the whole damn thing over to me, and that if I wanted anything or needed any help, all I had to do was call

him. He was as good as his word. I got the YMCA to send out tours to all the camps and bases in our sector. I also organized the 3rd Army Stock Company, composed of professionals who happened to be in uniform. We staged first-rate dramas, comedies, and musicals. I directed and occasionally acted, and we toured all over Germany. Those were fine times. We took over Fest Hall, a huge, beautiful auditorium in Coblenz, and I turned part of the interior into a theatre. We built a stage with a proscenium arch, a fly loft for the scenery, a lightboard—everything I needed. I had no thought then of a career in show business, but unwittingly I was getting the best apprenticeship I could have had."

After a year in Coblenz, Berkeley began to get restless. Like most civilian-soldiers, he wanted to go home. He wrote to the Adjutant General of the 3rd Army pleading his case, pointing out his record of duty, the length of time he had served, and that his mother was aging and needed her only surviving family member.

Actually, Gertrude Berkeley had been acting in New York, but she was sixty and doubtless wanted to be reunited with Busby. The Adjutant General sympathized with the request and Busby was soon proceeding to the embarkation base at St.. Nazaire, France, to be assigned space on a ship to America. At St. Nazaire, the commanding officer greeted him warmly, "Lieutenant, the men here badly need entertainment. If you don't have to go back right away, I think it would be a splendid idea if you would remain here for a while and organize a stock company. Then I'll put you on a boat and send you home. All right?" Berkeley had little choice but to accept. He organized the entertainment expected of him, and recalls that at one engagement they played to an audience of ten thousand soldiers.

Berkeley badgered the commanding officer until he was finally assigned a passage. As a last duty he was given a "filler company," a group of some two hundred men who had to be readied for sailing. Berkeley got his company ready in record time, but it turned out to be the usual army game of "hurry up and wait." Noticing that his name was listed on a boat about to sail, Berkeley handed over his company to a fellow lieutenant and got on the boat. "I was scared stiff about them finding out that I had assigned my company to another officer. I went to the hold of the ship, picked out a hammock, and stayed there until we were out of the harbor. Not long after that an orderly came to me and said I was to report to the C.O. I thought I'd had it. That was it—they'd caught up with me. The C.O. grilled me—was I this, had I done that. I thought I was about to be shot when he said, 'Well, in view of your experience, I want you to be the entertainment officer of this ship.' I put on as good a show as I could every night of the week, and when that boat docked in New York, I was the first one off. I literally ran down the gangplank."

Actor's Equity

Still in uniform with several days to go before being mustered out, Berkeley was in New York, walking through the theatrical district with his mother. They happened to meet director John Cromwell, an old friend of hers. "He greeted us warmly and asked what I was going to do when I got out of the Army. I had to admit that I had no plans. (My friend's father, the shoe manufacturer, had died and his company dissolved.) He looked at me rather quizzically and said, 'I'm putting out a road company of *The Man Who Came Back* and I need an actor about your age and size.'

"Mother said, 'No, John, I don't want Busby going on the stage,' but Cromwell was persuasive and she finally agreed to let me audition. I got the part, and after further persuasion from Cromwell, my mother gave in. Two days later I was discharged and we went into rehearsal. I played that part with the touring company for a whole year!"

Busby Berkeley enjoyed the tour. His mother traveled with him, coaching him in the craft of acting. "She was my toughest critic. I got good notices in the press and good audience response, but she still took my work apart, line by line. I remember coming off the stage one night after five curtain calls and cockily saying to her, 'What do you think of that?' She gave me a cold stare. 'Do you really want to know what I think? I think you're the worst dramatic actor I've ever seen.'

"Infuriated, I stalked off to my dressing room. While I was changing, I thought over what she said and it began to make sense—I really wasn't a dramatic actor, but I was good at comedy, I could make people laugh. I decided that this drama was my last."

The run of *The Man Who Came Back* ended and Berkeley discovered what every actor knows—having been a success in a play doesn't guarantee your next job. He went to New York and looked around for work. Hearing that producers Jones and Green were sending out a road company of their Broadway revue *Hitchy-Koo of 1923,* Berkeley landed a double-barreled job—assistant stage manager and actor in several sketches with the star comic Raymond Hitchcock.

Next came *Muchio Ito's Pin Wheel Revue* at the Little Theatre in New York. Berkeley played four small parts, three of them requiring completely different make-up and costumes—a South Seas native, a black deckhand, and a clown.

During the summers of the early 1920's Berkeley produced and directed musical shows using local talent, for Women's Clubs and local charities around New York.

It was characteristic that he would do just about anything, if it was wild and improbable. One summer while directing a local show in Paterson, New Jersey, he went up in a small biplane with an ace pilot as a publicity stunt. "As we flew over the city, I would get out of the cockpit, walk along the bottom wing, sit down, lock my legs around the end strut, and fall backwards. While I was hanging upside down, the plane was dipping and I would release balloons with tickets in them over the town." This fearlessness served Berkeley later in Hollywood, when he would stroll sixty feet up along the rafters of sound stages to plot his choreography.

Madam Lucy

In the fall of 1923, Berkeley landed a part in a revival of the musical *Irene* by walking up to producer James Montgomery and telling him he wanted to be in the show. Montgomery was amused by Berkeley's direct manner and asked him what part he would like. "I told him I was willing to play any of them. He replied, 'Do you think you could do Madam Lucy?' It was the big comedy part—an effeminate fashion designer. I immediately said, 'Of course.' I got the part and played Madam Lucy for the next three years of my life."

As Madam Lucy, Berkeley outlasted several actresses who played Irene. The third year, the beautiful Irene Dunne had the part, making her first major stage appearance. "She was a joy to work with, and would 'break up' if something happened that wasn't in the script. One night I entered in my grandiose manner as Madam Lucy, took her hand to kiss, and left her holding a raw oyster. That cracked her up for about two minutes on stage."

The part of Madam Lucy finally palled and he turned down the chance to repeat it for a fourth year. He had made up his mind to be a director. Signing with a stock company in Somerville, Massachusetts, at a fraction of the salary he had been getting as Madam Lucy, he had the unlimited opportunity both to direct and to act in a great variety of plays.

Seduction

The name Busby Berkeley gradually began to register in the entertainment world as a performer and director. Directing a company in Baltimore in 1926, Berkeley showed the kind of enterprise that would take him to the top. "We had a good company but we were playing way out on St. Charles Street, and people didn't want to go that far to see a show. The manager came to see me and said we would have to close—something I wanted to avoid at all costs. I knew he had written a play, an indifferent piece called *The White Sheik.* I saw how it could be hoked up. A show, *Simon Called Peter,* was running in Baltimore at that time, doing great business. I went to see it and discovered why: in one scene the villain tore the heroine's dress and exposed a bare breast. If that's what people wanted, I figured I could do better. I went around to all the dance halls in Baltimore and found eight beautiful girls who had no objection to appearing almost nude. From New York I got Alyn King, the famous Ziegfeld beauty. I renamed the show *Seduction* and covered my stage with four truckloads of sand. In the meantime, I wrote the publicity, with lines like—'See the Passionate Nautche Dancers of the Desert . . . See a Woman's Soul Laid Bare to Love!' I had eight dancing girls slithering around the stage in see-through veils, and at one performance I had my villain rip Alyn King's dress and expose both breasts! We played to packed houses for weeks."

Berkeley next turned to Somerville and staged two musicals, *Molly Darling* and *Up She Goes,* which he produced and directed, and in which he played the comedy lead. By now offers of employment were coming in and Berkeley chose only the jobs that appealed to him. He stuck to musical comedies he knew and drew a double salary, averaging $250 a week as director and the same amount as comedy lead.

The press began to take notice. He had long been collecting good reviews for his comic acting, but now there were references to the staging of his dance routines, "his intricate counter-rhythms and his unusual, creative style."

Broadway Calls

At last came the call from Broadway. Berkeley was hired to stage *Holka Polka,* which began as a Czech operetta and was now being refurbished as a Broadway musical, with extra songs by Harry Ruby and Bert Kalmer. *Holka Polka* was not a great success, but Berkeley's dance routines were praised.

But show business is feast or famine and after his first New York run, he waited in vain for another offer. He lived at the St. Andrews Hotel, low on funds, but trying to keep up appearances.

Berkeley had an extroverted manner and a casual attitude toward money. Although he had earned good money for several years, nothing had been saved. He gave a generous allowance to his mother, and the rest was spent cavalierly. His pride was too enormous even to admit to his mother that he was down to his last few dollars.

After weeks of inactivity, Berkeley got a message to come to a theatre in Brooklyn—a producer was worried about dance routines and wanted advice. Taking the subway to Brooklyn, he realized he didn't even have a nickel to get back. "After I had seen the show, the producer sheepishly told me he was sorry to have dragged me all the way to Brooklyn, but his partner had already hired another dance director. I made light of it and bravely said good night. I walked the entire night, got to my hotel about eleven in the morning, and dropped into bed exhausted. Sometime in the late afternoon the telephone rang. It was the Brooklyn producer telling me he had talked his partner out of hiring the other man and the job was mine." The show was *Castles in the Air,* which gave Berkeley several weeks' work.

In those days, the dance director was dismissed a week or so after the show had been staged. The job called for a man to devise the dancing, rehearse it, and leave once it was working. Berkeley realized the value of being both a performer and a dance director —the performer stayed with the show. He staged the musical numbers for *Lady Do* and when, on the second night of the run, the lead baritone fell ill, utility man Berkeley went on in his place.

Next came the job of creating and staging the dances in *Sweet Lady,* which collapsed before it reached Broadway because of lack of funds. The show featured a young English dancer named Archie Leach, better known today as Cary Grant. *Sweet Lady* did, however, bring Berkeley to the attention of a good agent, Louis Shurr.

Knowing that Rodgers and Hart were about to stage a new musical, *A Connecticut Yankee,* and that it would call for especially good choreography, Shurr praised his new client to producer Lew Fields. Fields knew Busby's work and agreed to a contract. It was the kind of break every artist needs, a chance for him to reach a new level in his career.

Busby Berkeley operated very largely on nerve. He had acquired a reputation as a choreographer, yet he had never studied the art and had never taken a dancing lesson. His bluff had never been called, and so far the game was successful, but on *A Connecticut Yankee* he had reason to worry. "The second act opened with Queen Guinevere's dancing class in the castle. I thought it would be a good ploy to start the scene with the Queen teaching the class the first five positions of dance. The trouble was I didn't even know the first position, let alone the others. So I walked around the stage rubbing my head and pretending I was thinking up something. I said to one of the girls, 'I think I'll have the Queen start off by showing the first position.' She said, 'Oh, you mean this,' and pointed her feet in a certain way. I looked out of the corner of my eye to see what she was doing and then pointed to another girl. 'Second position,' and so on. In this way, and without their knowing it, I learned the first five positions of dance."

A Connecticut Yankee opened at the Vanderbilt Theatre in New York, November 3, 1927, and ran for 421 performances, in addition to a London run and a touring company. The many merits of the show were lauded by the critics. One New York critic wrote, "A new dance director has been born on Broadway." The offers began to come in. Berkeley's next job was choreographing *The Golden Dawn,* a rearrangement of an Emmerich Kalman operetta, followed by *The White Eagle,* a Rudolf Friml operetta based on *The Squaw Man.*

The year 1928 was a busy one for Busby Berkeley with five Broadway musical comedies to be choreographed. Richard Rodgers, Lorenz Hart, and Lew Fields had been pleased with what Berkeley did for *A Connecticut Yankee,* and they offered him a similar position on *Present Arms,* a lighter vehicle than *Yankee* and more comedic. Although it wasn't as good or as successful as *Yankee, Present Arms* turned out to be a bigger personal venture for Berkeley, because after Lew Fields dismissed the actor playing the comedy lead during the out-of-town tryout, he offered the part to Berkeley, who played it on Broadway for nine weeks. The story is set in Hawaii and concerns a young U.S. Marine's attempts to woo and win an aristocratic English girl. Berkeley played a Marine sergeant, and both his acting and dance direction won plaudits.

Stage Fright

The opening night of *Present Arms* is precious to Berkeley, as it also was to Lorenz Hart. "I launched into my first song, 'You Took Advantage of Me,' and after the first chorus my mind went blank. I couldn't remember a line, but I had to keep on singing. I concocted some lines like:

> When I was walking down the street,
> I saw a little bird who called tweet-tweet,
> I shook my head and said instead,
> 'Cause you took advantage of me.

It was awful, but I got through it; I can still see poor Larry Hart running up and down in the wings almost apoplectic. He already had a reputation for witty, poetic lyrics, and here I was ruining his marvelous lines. But I drew a lot of laughs from the audience that night and he later forgave me."

Berkeley had to leave *Present Arms* in order to prepare his next show, *The Earl Carroll Vanities of 1928*. At the same time he organized his own stock company, The Berkeley Players, as a sideline venture in Plainfield, New Jersey. The company did well, but Berkeley realized he had overextended himself and after a few months he closed it. Since he had long wanted his own company, this was a disappointment, but the acclaim he had found on Broadway was too important to jeopardize.

The Earl Carroll Vanities of 1928.

The Berkeley Technique

Busby Berkeley was often asked how he devised his dance routines and where he got his ideas. Berkeley has never been able to answer these questions—any explanation of how he did what he did would have to come from others.

The best analysis was published in *The New York Times*, July 22, 1928. The account provides an insight into the Berkeley mystique. It would have been just as valid twenty years later as a comment on his films:

> Busby Berkeley assumes the mantle of a kind of modern prophet, though he himself probably hasn't found it out yet. What Berkeley did in *A Connecticut Yankee*, and even to a greater extent in *Present Arms*, was to discover a new and sound basis upon which to build for novelty. He delved into the actual rhythmic structure of jazz to a degree that has not before

been attempted. If there can be such a thing as "high-brow" jazz dancing, his creations cannot escape being so catalogued.

> The first act of *Present Arms* contains complicated and subtle rhythms that many a trained musician or a trained artist dancer would find next to impossible to perform. In many cases the dancers are required to execute contrary rhythms, and in one number, they are called upon to perform simultaneously, two rhythms counter to each other, and also, the music. A musical director who worked with Berkeley is quoted as saying that he did not dare to watch the dancing, for fear he could not move his baton to the required beat of the score. In *The Earl Carroll Vanities*, now in rehearsal, there are similar difficulties involved, such as counting five against four, then three against four, and a third rhythm still to be added with the arms when the two have been mastered.

> He creates none of these dances in advance; in fact, his inspiration seems to come from having the girls in front of him on the stage ready for work.

The Earl Carroll Vanities of 1928 was a considerable success and resulted in offers of other jobs. In quick succession came *Good Boy*, with songs by Ruby and Kalmar, *Rainbow*, an ambitious musical play by Laurence Stallings, with music by Vincent Youmans and lyrics by Oscar Hammerstein II, and *Hello Daddy*, with songs by Jimmy McHugh and Dorothy Fields.

In September of 1928 Berkeley got a call to see J. J. Shubert and his brother Lee, the wealthiest theatrical producers in New York, who operated a combine that staged every kind of dramatic and musical production. They also owned many of the theatres on Broadway. Their machine ran like clockwork, Lee Shubert producing the dramatic shows and J.J. the musicals. J.J. was preparing to bring a revue called *Pleasure Bound*, starring Jack Pearl and Phil Baker, to New York. He was not pleased with it and hired Berkeley to give it some sparkle. "We rehearsed for a week in Newark, and then took it to Cleveland for some more restaging. In Cleveland, I got an urgent call from Arthur Hammerstein telling me he was doing Rudolf Friml's operetta, *The Wild Rose*. The company was playing Springfield, Massachusetts, and the show needed fixing. As soon as I finished *Pleasure Bound*, I went to Springfield. I suggested that Hammerstein close the show for a week, work on restaging, and then rehearse in New York. *Pleasure Bound* opened on Broadway just a week ahead of *The Wild Rose*, and I had become known as Doctor Buzz, the Show Fixer." Berkeley also became known as one of the Big Four among Broadway dance directors; the others were Sammy Lee, Bobby Connolly, and Seymour Felix. While the "Mr. Fix-it" reputation was flattering, Berkeley wanted to direct and produce Broadway shows.

A Night in Venice

His first Broadway show as a director was *A Night in Venice*, a revue with songs by several composers, starring comedian Ted Healy and The Three Stooges. It opened in Philadelphia, then came to New York for a long run at the Shubert Theatre.

During these years of success on Broadway, Berkeley had been living with his mother in an apartment on Park Avenue and Ninety-first Street. Knowing her son to be a spendthrift, Gertrude Berkeley persuaded him to invest in property. "I bought an estate with a twenty-four-room house in Dover, New Hampshire, and moved Mother into it. She collected antiques and I indulged her. As long as I had money, she could have anything she wanted. After the way she had suffered and worked for so many years, I was glad to let her have anything she fancied. I was too dumb at the time to realize that her antique collecting was also a form of investment and that she was doing it deliberately."

While in Philadelphia with *A Night in Venice*, Berkeley met the woman who became his first wife. "I dropped in to see another show and saw an actress named Esther Muir. She was a beautiful, statuesque blonde, and I was smitten from the moment she walked on stage. Afterwards, I went backstage, introduced myself, and immediately started a campaign of dating and courting. We continued this into New York and finally got engaged, but it was impossible to set a date for the wedding because we were both too busy. Some time later, I got a cable from J. J. Shubert telling me to join him in London, where he was auditioning European talent. Esther got out of her show, and she, my mother, and I went together. In London we had a falling-out which resulted in Esther's going back to America on one boat and Mother and I on another. Then I was given my next assignment, staging and directing *The Duchess of Chicago*.

"Again I was up to my ears in work, with every waking hour spent arranging and rehearsing the show, but I kept phoning Esther. She said she would see me only if we agreed to set a date for our wedding. I figured the only date I could aim for would be during the show's tryout in Baltimore. At one point J. J. Shubert saw me rushing out of the theatre and asked where I was going. As I ran off I told him I was on my way to City Hall to get a marriage license, and he yelled after me, 'What a damn fool you are!' After City Hall, I ran to a jeweler, then rushed to the station to meet Esther, and zoomed back to the theatre in time for the curtain. We were married in the theatre that night, with a surprise party thrown by J.J. right on the stage."

Unfortunately, *The Duchess of Chicago* opened to poor notices in New York and closed after a few performances. J. J. next hired Berkeley to stage the musical numbers in an elaborate revue starring the celebrated nightclub personality Texas Guinan. Called *Broadway Nights*, it opened on July 15, 1929, and had a modest run. In negotiating his contract for *Broadway Nights*, Berkeley said he would do it provided the Shuberts later gave him a show of his own to direct.

The Producer

Shubert gave him his first assignment as a producer—the French farce *The Street Singer*. Rather than hire a director and a choreographer, Berkeley undertook the complete job himself, becoming the first producer in the American theatre to be responsible for directing a musical containing his own created and staged dances, and establishing a precedent for talented men like Jerome Robbins, Michael Kidd, and Gower Champion many years later.

The Street Singer ran for a full season and brought Berkeley first-rate notices. Gilbert Seldes wrote:

> The dances Busby Berkeley arranged for *The Street Singer* were so numerous, intricate, exciting and well done that nothing else in the show mattered ... the novelty and the assurance of the entire chorus body were all exciting and gave specific character to the show.

Other critics referred to Berkeley's dancers as "about the fastest-stepping throng of pretty girls ever to enliven a stage," and remarked that "his tireless, peppy, pulchritudinous chorus won salvos of applause."

Shubert called Berkeley and instructed him to be at the theatre one midnight to audition a new score by Sigmund Romberg. "When I got there I found a twenty-four-piece orchestra in the pit and Romberg himself standing ready to conduct. Usually to present a new score, the composer knocks it out on a piano with his lyricist doing the singing, and seldom do either of them do justice to their work. This was not the way Romberg did things; he paid to have the score orchestrated and he hired and paid the orchestra. Shubert asked me how I liked it, and all I could say was it sounded fine, it had that typical Romberg style and verve, full of melodies. Shubert said, 'Glad you like it because you're going to stage and direct it.' The result was *Nina Rose*, a dramatic operetta set in Peru, and although it didn't turn out to be a Romberg classic, it was a pleasant show and we had a respectable run."

When his contract with the Shuberts ran out, Berkeley declined their offer to renew for a more attractive proposition from impresario Lew Leslie. Leslie had been enormously successful with his all-Negro shows, *Shuffle Along* and *Blackbirds of 1928*, and he wanted Berkeley to stage his *International Review*, which promised to be a highly successful musical. Berkeley accepted. He had one more show to do before taking on the job with Leslie—staging the songs and dances for *The 9:15 Revue*, remembered only because it contained Harold Arlen's first song, "Get Happy." *Lew Leslie's International Review* starred Gertrude Lawrence, along with an excellent score by Jimmy McHugh and Dorothy Fields. Two of their songs for this show became standards—"Exactly Like You" and "On the Sunny Side of the Street." Berkeley recalls that in the orchestra pit were three young musicians named Benny Goodman, Harry James, and Tommy Dorsey.

How about *Whoopee?*

While working on *Lew Leslie's International Review*, Busby Berkeley was approached by The William Morris Agency and asked if he would be interested in going to Hollywood. "I told them I was not at all interested. I had seen a few film musicals and I hadn't been impressed; they looked terribly static and restricted. But the Morris people kept hounding me. I finally said, 'All right, you get me a great star, a great producer, and a great property and I might consider it.' They replied, 'You want a great star? How about Eddie Cantor?' I nodded. 'You want a great producer? How about Florenz Ziegfeld and Sam Goldwyn together?' I blinked. 'You want a great property? How about *Whoopee?*' With a barrage like that there wasn't much I could do but agree. I doubted that such a deal existed, but the Morris people invited me to their office to talk with Goldwyn on the telephone. Goldwyn confirmed that he had indeed bought *Whoopee*, which had been a great success on Broadway, with Cantor starring and Ziegfeld producing, and that Cantor and Ziegfeld had been signed for the film and wanted me to direct the musical sequences. All that remained now was to settle on a salary. I was then getting $1000 a week in New York and I figured if they wanted me in Hollywood I could get $1500 a week. But Goldwyn was a shrewd dealer, and $1000 a week was as much as he was prepared to pay. As I was haggling with him, someone nudged me with a cane, 'Go on, Buzz, take the thousand. What do you care? They've got golf courses out there five min-

Young Busby Berkeley on the first set of his first movie, *Whoopee*. Photo by Fred Zimmerman.

utes from the studio, the ocean at your back door, beautiful beaches, sunshine every day. Take the thousand.' I turned around and saw Al Jolson. With his prodding, I accepted Goldwyn's offer, and I often kidded him for talking me into taking less than I might have got if he hadn't been there."

With *Lew Leslie's International Review* successfully launched and running, and his contract completed, Berkeley and his bride took off for the West Coast. He had been in the theatre for almost a decade, during the glamorous, pulsating Roaring Twenties. In the previous three years Berkeley had been associated with twenty Broadway shows. It was Spring 1930 and he was about to enter another fantastic era—the Hollywood of the 1930's.

The Hollywood Years

The One-eyed Box

Mr. and Mrs. Busby Berkeley were met at the Los Angeles depot in traditional Hollywood fashion by representatives of the Goldwyn Studio and The William Morris Agency. Installed in the Hollywood Roosevelt Hotel, they were taken to the studio to meet Samuel Goldwyn. "He was very cordial and said he felt happy to have me with him on his first musical venture. He asked me what my first step would be and I told him 'Girls.' He smiled at this and told me the choice was entirely mine. Like everyone else, I doubt if he considered picking girls for the chorus more work than one would think. Actually, you had to look for more than pretty faces and shapely limbs. The girls needed intelligence, coordination, and the ability to understand intricate routines—plus good endurance, since the work was long and tiring. In choosing girls I found I could tell a great deal about them from their eyes—something people are unwilling to believe. Among the first girls I picked for *Whoopee* were Betty Grable, then only fifteen, Virginia Bruce, and Claire Dodd."

Goldwyn advised Berkeley to spend several weeks wandering around the studios, observing. Berkeley knew nothing about film-making, but it wasn't something he was going to admit. "I realized, of course, that the technique was entirely different from the stage. In pictures you see everything through the eye of the camera. Unlike the theatre, where your eyes can roam at will, the director and his cameramen decide where the viewer will look. It was obvious to me that film musicals so far had been disappointing because no one thought of imaginative things to do with the camera. With my reputation as a man who came up with unique ideas, I now desperately tried to think of some. My total ignorance of photography and the completely alien environment made it difficult to keep up a façade of assurance.

"The art director of *Whoopee*, Richard Day, happened to notice me looking at a camera with obvious puzzlement and gave me a piece of advice that helped me greatly. 'Buzz, they try to make a big secret out of that little box, but it's no mystery at all. All you have to remember is that the camera has only one eye, not two. You can see a lot with two eyes but hold a hand over one and it cuts your area of vision.' This was very simple advice but it made all the difference. I started planning my numbers with one eye in mind. It was then customary for the film's director to take over when it came to the actual shooting of the numbers, and I was supposed to step aside. I had never worked that way on Broadway and I wasn't going to work like that now. I went to Goldwyn and told him I wanted to film my own numbers. He hedged and asked me if I thought I could handle it. I replied, 'Mr. Goldwyn, I don't think I can, I *know* I can.' This kind of confidence seemed to impress him and I got his permission. When I walked on the set to start shooting, I saw four cameras and four crews. This was something else I didn't know about, and I asked my assistant for an explanation. He told me the standard technique was for a routine to be filmed from four directions and that the cutter would assemble the shots, make a selection, and put the scene together. With another show of confidence I announced, 'Oh? Well, it's not my technique. I use only one camera, so let the others go.' I finally got my way, and during my entire career in films I have never used more than one camera on anything. My idea was to plan every shot and edit in the camera."

Berkeley used his now famous overhead shots for the first time in *Whoopee*. He also used a technique that was a first in movie musicals: close-ups of the chorus girls. Watching him work, a mystified Sam Goldwyn asked him why he was doing this. "Well, we've got all these beautiful girls in the picture. Why not let the public see them?" The logic was immediately apparent to Goldwyn.

Busby Berkeley believed he would be as busy in Hollywood as he had been on Broadway. Though *Whoopee* was well received, by late 1930 it was obvious that musicals in general were failing at the box office. The deluge of the first frantic year had dried up; musical films were expensive and difficult to make and the producers hesitated to make any more. After he had finished the Goldwyn picture, Berkeley was signed by Paramount, but he found himself sitting in his office week after week with no work. Billy Rose, whose Diamond Horseshoe nightclub was prospering, called Berkeley and asked him if he could come East to work on a musical comedy. Paramount readily agreed to a leave of absence, and Berkeley went to New York to stage *Sweet and Low*. Starring Fannie Brice and George Jessel, with music by Harry Warren, the show opened on November 17, 1930. Its best song, "Would You Like to Take a Walk?" became one of Warren's many standards. Not long after this, Warren himself gave up Broadway and became closely associated with Busby Berkeley in Hollywood.

Once *Sweet and Low* no longer needed his services, Berkeley returned to Paramount where he continued to do nothing but pick up his weekly paycheck. He and Paramount agreed to sever the contract and make a settlement. Berkeley—a musical specialist in an industry no longer interested in producing musicals—had to start looking around for work. The first thing to come his way was the job of arranging the dances for *Kiki*, a Mary Pickford film which she didn't like when it was completed and didn't want released. By this time *Whoopee* had done so well that Goldwyn decided to make another Eddie Cantor picture, with Berkeley again doing the musical numbers. It was called *Palmy Days*, and with some months to go before its release, Berkeley was again job-hunting. He had made up his mind to return to New York, but tells how Mervyn LeRoy talked him out of leaving. "Mervyn had been brought in to direct parts of *Palmy Days* when Edward Sutherland, the director, was called away on another assignment. Mervyn told me he admired my ideas and was absolutely confident that musicals would come back. He was very persuasive, so I stayed on. Again, weeks of inactivity and more wondering whether I was doing the right thing. Nothing came along in films, so I went to work for the Los Angeles production house of Fanchon and Marco, which specialized in producing stage prologues for first-run movie houses. Incidentally, Fanchon and Marco were the inspiration for *Footlight Parade*. I did a few things for them and then was called back into the film business as dance director for *Flying High, Night World*, and *Bird of Paradise*. These jobs were not particularly inspiring, and I was about to pack up and head for New York when I got a call from Goldwyn to do another Eddie Cantor picture, *The Kid From Spain*. I jumped at it. By the time we finished it, there were signs that the public was becoming more receptive to musical films, and Darryl Zanuck managed to talk Warner Brothers into one last fling at a large-scale musical. Through Mervyn LeRoy, Zanuck called me in and asked if I would create the musical sequences of *42nd Street*." The rest is history.

Berkeley instructing chorines.

February 10, 1934. Busby Berkeley and second wife, Merna Kennedy, leaving the First Methodist Church, Hollywood, California.

Berkeley's Brides

During his first year in Hollywood, Berkeley and his wife found their life together not what they had hoped for. They separated and divorced on the grounds of incompatibility. It was a pattern that would repeat itself over the next six years. Busby Berkeley married no less than six times, and only in his last marriage did he find the right partner. Each of Berkeley's brides found him devoted to his work, making a normal home life impossible, as working hours stretched from early in the morning to late at night—occasionally right through the night. Although soft-hearted and easy-going with women, Berkeley was at times amazingly casual with them and frequently absent-minded. His friends have said that he was an easy mark for ambitious women and that he was given to impulsive proposals of marriage.

With his first marriage dissolved, Berkeley bought an expensive home in Beverly Hills for his mother. She advised him to invest his money in real estate and continued to build up her antique collection. Gertrude Berkeley had every reason to feel proud of

her son. He had reached a level of success which brought him great acclaim and a large salary. She could read in Louella Parsons's column:

> Busby Berkeley has revolutionized musical comedies and made it possible for the screen to feature girl revues comparable with the Ziegfeld Follies. It was Berkeley who saw the possibilities in photographical dance ensembles.

In reviewing *The Gold Diggers of 1933*, Relma Morin of the Los Angeles *Record* wrote:

> It's a dazzling, eye paralyzing, ear tickling creation that makes all the other musical films look like Delaney Street peep shows. The star of the picture is the gentleman who does not appear in it. Busby Berkeley, the geometrically-minded lad who created the dance sequences, has done a perfectly amazing job.

While working on *The Gold Diggers of 1933* Berkeley became acquainted with actress Merna Kennedy, who had appeared with Charles Chaplin in *The Circus*. Says Berkeley, "It was a whirlwind courtship and a typical Hollywood wedding. Jack Warner was my best man, and many of the stars from the studio turned up. They staged a huge champagne party for us, and then we left for a honeymoon in San Francisco. While courting Merna I had the luck to become acquainted with her friends Etta Dunn and Leonard Judd, who later married. They were always my staunchest friends."

Married to Merna, Berkeley sold his Beverly Hills home and bought property his mother had found, an estate in Redlands, California, with a large house, pool, stables, and fourteen acres of orange groves. She occupied this house while Berkeley and his bride leased another in Beverly Hills.

The Berkeley career now moved into high gear, with one smash musical after another. The work was constant and exacting and the Berkeley mind seldom rested. "A lot of ideas came to me in the bath. I used to lie in a warm tub for half an hour each morning before going to the studio and I found it my best period of inspiration. This fact became well-known around Warner's and any time I came in with enthusiasm, people would yell, 'Watch out, Berkeley's just come from the bathtub.' Before rehearsing the big musical routines, I would gather the girls around a blackboard, and as in a classroom, have them sit and watch me explain the movements with diagrams. This always captured their interest— explaining the purpose of the routine, where the camera would be, where they would be. I would also draw a sketch of the final shot. This procedure was especially helpful in doing the overhead shots of the complicated patterns."

The Million Dollar Dance Director

Busby Berkeley's nickname, The Million Dollar Dance Director, was not so much a reference to his expensive musical creations as to the money spent by Warner Brothers and Samuel Goldwyn in a legal hassle over his services. Berkeley had a commitment to Goldwyn which Warner's had taken over when they signed Berkeley to a seven-year contract. While he was doing *Footlight Parade*, Goldwyn told him that he was expected to start work immediately on another Eddie Cantor musical, *Roman Scandals*. Goldwyn was unmoved by Berkeley's protestations that since he hadn't yet finished the elaborate routines of *Footlight Parade*, he wouldn't be able to report to the Goldwyn studio for some weeks. Goldwyn brought suit against Warner's for breach of contract, which resulted in a trial at the Superior Court in Los Angeles. The trial lasted several years and involved two expensive law firms. Goldwyn lost the case and had to wait until Berkeley had completed *Footlight Parade* before he could undertake *Roman Scandals*. The court action cost the studios a good deal of money, but the publicity was worth every penny!

Berkeley worked at a mad pace during his first two years with Warner's. He was involved in eight films during that period, all but one of them big musicals requiring many elaborate routines. Fame came to Busby Berkeley, but he paid the price in the collapse of his marriage to Merna. Without doubt she was justified in her familiar cry that he was married to his work. They certainly had not spent much time together in the year since they had been married. Of course, Berkeley was the Boy Wonder of the studio, and if pounding his brains for ideas and exhausting himself putting them into effect contributed to the disintegration of his marriage, his employers didn't care, as long as he came up with what they wanted.

The frequent suggestion that his life on Broadway and in Hollywood must have been full of fun and excitement brings a wry smile to Busby Berkeley's face. "There was fun and there certainly was excitement, but what I mostly remember is stress and strain and exhaustion. I worried about being able to come up with new ideas, and then I worried about how they would go over with the public. My musical routines for Warner's used to average $100,000—about $10,000 per minute of screen time —big money in those days. When you're spending money like that, you have the executives from the front office breathing down your neck. It was grueling and sometimes terrifying, because you couldn't give way to despair or lack of confidence. As Browning said, 'Self-confidence is the first requisite of great understandings.' If Browning had worked in Hollywood in its heyday, he might have added other requisites. As anyone in the entertainment business knows, becoming successful is not nearly as hard as staying successful."

Reviewers seemed to feel challenged for words and phrases to describe Busby Berkeley. He was called "an optometrist extraordinary," "a kaleidoscopic genius," "a marvel of ingenuity," and "a master of visual motion." Berkeley had a right to feel on top of the world.

The elation did not last.

Manslaughter

In September of 1935, Berkeley attended a party in Pacific Palisades given by William Koenig, production manager at Warner's. He had to leave early to keep an appointment with bandleader Gus Arnheim in Santa Monica. As he drove along the twisting Pacific Coast Highway, the left front tire of his roadster blew out and he careened into the path of oncoming traffic. In the resulting head-on collision, two people were killed instantly, and a third died later. Busby was dragged unconscious from his burning car.

Berkeley was tried three times on charges of manslaughter. Two trials resulted in a hung jury. At a third trial a verdict of "not guilty" was handed down. Jerry Giesler, the well-known Hollywood attorney who defended celebrities, had shown the difficulty of driving that stretch of coastal highway and that a blown-out tire on a small roadster would make the car impossible to control. With sworn testimony from guests at the party, Giesler proved that Berkeley was not drunk when he set out for Santa Monica.

The trials were emotionally harrowing and physically exhausting, because Berkeley was working on film schedules that could not be altered. He recalls that on the first day of his third trial, he had to arrive in court at nine after working the previous night until two in the morning on a Dick Powell sequence in *Stage Struck*.

Gertrude Berkeley with Busby immediately after his acquittal.

Berkeley had another good reason for working—the expenses of the trials and the various fees came to almost $100,000. "I was lucky that I had so much work because it helped keep my mind off the accident. Even though I was found innocent, it was a shocking and terribly depressing thing to have been involved in the death of three people. I think it was the heavy work commitment of the time that saved my sanity."

Busby Berkeley's career with Warner's continued to escalate. He was working on an average of four pictures a year. The large-scale musicals became fewer, partly because the cost of making them grew appreciably greater and partly because Warner Brothers shrewdly gauged the changing tastes of the public. The frothy backstage musical was perfect escapist entertainment for the early years of the Depression, but as economic conditions improved, the public expected musicals with a little more reality. By 1937, the tide had turned; *Varsity Show* and *Hollywood Hotel* were the last of the gigantic Warner spectacular song-and-dance numbers. Afterwards they produced only occasional musicals, and these stressed romance and comedy. The changes suited Berkeley. He had made it known to Warner's that he wanted to direct, and further, that he did not want to be limited to musicals. He proved himself a capable director with his last film under contract—the dramatic and realistic *They Made Me a Criminal,* a non-musical entirely different from those that had made his name famous.

John Garfield in a scene from *They Made Me a Criminal,* with The Dead End Kids.

MGM

While *They Made Me a Criminal* was in production, the subject of Berkeley's contract came up. "They wanted to renew it, but without the increase previously agreed upon. At the same time, my manager, Mike Levee, was urging me to leave Warner's because he thought I could do better freelance. I took his advice, and the day after I left Warner's I was at MGM."

MGM needed Berkeley to do a spectacular ending for their Jeanette MacDonald picture, *Broadway Serenade.* The rest of the film had been made and MacDonald was committed to an immediate concert tour. For the finale MGM had acquired the rights to the Tchaikovsky song "None But the Lonely Heart," and Herbert Stothart had arranged an elaborate symphonic and choral treatment. The problem was to invent a suitable visual finale. Their satisfaction with Berkeley's solution resulted in a contract on a yearly renewal basis. In accepting it, Berkeley stipulated that he would be adviser and dance director on musicals, but his primary function would be directing.

Berkeley acquired more real estate. He bought a palatial home on West Adams Boulevard in Los Angeles and moved in with his mother, now in her eighties, but still watching over her son's financial affairs and her large collection of rare antiques and *objets d'art.* "It looked more like a museum than a home, but it made her happy and that's all I cared

The grounds of Berkeley's home on Adams Boulevard in Los Angeles.

about. As she was confined to a wheelchair, I turned the basement into a theatre and installed a projection booth so she could see my pictures. She still had a shrewd business mind, insisting that we keep the estate in Redlands, just as we had kept the house in Dover, New Hampshire. I took her advice, and in years to come, I was glad I did."

The next four years at MGM were profitable ones. There were three Mickey Rooney–Judy Garland musicals, *Babes in Arms, Strike Up the Band,* and *Babes on Broadway,* all of which were popular. He also did several comedies, arranged musical sequences for several of the famous studio musicals, and supervised portions of *Bitter Sweet* and *The Wizard of Oz.*

Berkeley's career went smoothly, except for his marriages. His third wife, Claire James, had won the beauty contest title of Miss California and later worked as an extra in films. They met at Warner's and they dated for two years, deciding to get married on the spur of the moment in Las Vegas. "I had a one-day break in a shooting schedule. We were married, but there was no connubial bliss. Poor Claire had never had a drink in her life, and the cocktail party after the ceremony knocked her out. She spent our wedding night unconscious until I woke her up the next morning in time to catch the plane to Los Angeles. I took her home to her mother.

A few days later, she called to say that she didn't want to be married, so it was annulled. That was number three."

Shortly after this dismal incident, Berkeley went to Louis B. Mayer and explained that he needed a vacation. "I told him that in all the time I had worked on Broadway and in Hollywood, I had never been away for a holiday. This surprised him, just as it surprised all the people who imagined I led a glamorous, gay life, and he agreed to give me a month off. I decided on a motor trip back East, taking Mother with me. We were both eager to see the old places again. The trip started off well, but as we drove through Oklahoma, the car hit a dip in the road and Mother was thrown from the back seat onto the floor. She tore the ligaments in one leg and had to be hospitalized for a week. I sent the car back to Los Angeles and we went on by train, with Mother carried on a stretcher. She was never able to walk again, but we saw the house in Dover and the other places that meant so much to her."

It was customary in the heyday of the big-studio system in Hollywood for companies to lend their talents to each other, usually for considerations other than money. A star, a writer, or a director might be lent to one studio in return for a similar service. Warner's had refused to let Busby Berkeley be used by other studios, because they didn't want anyone else profiting from his distinctive contributions. In 1943 MGM let Berkeley direct *The Gang's All Here* for Twentieth Century–Fox and then, in an ironic piece of horse trading, allowed Berkeley to go to Warner Brothers if Warner's would take over Joan Crawford's contract. MGM was dissatisfied with Crawford and figured several million dollars could be saved if she could be unloaded on another studio. It turned out to be an unwise move, because Joan Crawford did well at Warner's, winning an Oscar for *Mildred Pierce*.

Back at Warner's

Warner's welcomed Berkeley back and told him that if he could get out of his MGM contract they would sign him for five years at a higher salary. It was arranged, and Berkeley began what he thought would be another long and successful association with the studio. It was not to be. After directing *Cinderella Jones* in the early part of 1944, he was assigned an expensive treatment of the life of the famous Ziegfeld musical comedy star Marilyn Miller, but the project ran into problems of legal clearance and was shelved.

There was another stipulation in the new contract—Berkeley wanted not only to direct, but also to produce. Jack Warner, then in charge of production at the studio, had little interest in this, undoubtedly believing he could function best as a director. Berkeley now paid a price for his ambition. "I kept calling Jack's office, put off with messages saying that he was in conference or that he was off the lot. One day I impetuously told Jack's assistant that if Warner wouldn't see me, I wanted to be released from my contract. The next morning, I received a telegram from Jack Warner informing me that, as per my wishes, my contract with the studio was canceled."

New York Disaster

Busby Berkeley received several offers from other Hollywood producers, but the one he accepted came from songwriters Jule Styne and Sammy Cahn. They were writing the score for a Broadway musical and wanted to know if Berkeley would stage and direct it. Berkeley was more than interested, he was eager to get back to the stage and away from the film business. The show was *Glad to See You*, with Lupe Velez, Jane Withers, and Eddie Davis signed for the leads. Berkeley proceeded to New York with his mother and his secretary. He took a suite at the Savoy Plaza and engaged two nurses to attend his mother.

Berkeley's career had been going well for some twenty years—now the pendulum was about to swing the other way. After lining up his cast and crew for *Glad to See You*, and starting preliminary rehearsals, rumors of the producer's financial troubles began to circulate. Lupe Velez, known as The Mexican Spitfire, called Berkeley to her hotel, furiously complaining about her treatment since she had not been greeted at the station by newsmen, photographers, or flowers—in fact, there was not even a hotel room reserved for her. She ranted that the producer was no good and announced her immediate return to Hollywood, suggesting that Berkeley do the same. Lupe's defection was a blow. The show opened in Philadelphia to bad notices. The producer's financial problems turned out to be real and Berkeley, on the advice of counsel, terminated his contract. The show folded.

Although *Glad to See You* had a short run, it was long enough to bring about Berkeley's marriage to Myra Steffin, a member of the cast who had been a high-fashion model in New York, known as "the girl with the velvet skin." Their

marriage lasted only a few weeks and ended in annulment. Previous wives complained about Berkeley's devoting all his time to his work. Myra complained that he devoted all his time to worrying about finding work and about a mother who was nearing the end of her life.

Gertrude Berkeley still watched out for her son's interests. Well over eighty, she had insisted on going to Philadelphia with him, saying that she never missed one of his openings and did not intend to start now. This one would be her last. Since she knew her son was incapable of managing money, she suggested that he buy a house in Oklahoma City and a cattle ranch near Shawnee, Oklahoma. She had discovered these properties during her stay in the Oklahoma hospital. As directed, the properties were purchased in her name; her will named Busby as her only heir.

After their return to California, Gertrude Berkeley contracted pneumonia. Busby launched a fight for her life, locating a specialist in treating the disease, who was flown in from Oklahoma City. Responding to treatment, Gertrude was placed in a sanitarium, but she was so unhappy there that Berkeley had her brought home. Two nurses were in constant attendance, with daily visits from doctors. "I didn't realize what it was all costing until much later. One of the bad things about Los Angeles is that there are two sets of prices, one for ordinary citizens and one for those in the picture business. Since I wasn't working, the upkeep and taxes on our properties were burning up my capital."

Wife Number Five

At this point, Berkeley embarked upon yet another marriage. Wife number five was Marge Pemberton, a showgirl he had dated in previous years. "It was the worst possible time to get married, but Marge was very sympathetic and understanding, genuinely wanting to help. Not long after the wedding, the doctors told me my mother had terminal cancer. I wanted to stay with her as much as I could, so I asked Marge to move back with her parents until it was all over. Mother lingered for another nine months. It was a terrible period and almost deranged me. She died on June 14, 1946. I decided to take her back to Ohio to be buried beside my father. Marge came with me, but I told her she had best remain with her parents when we returned to Los Angeles—I knew I wasn't fit to be with at that time.

"I moved into a small house and asked my Japanese houseboy, Frank Honda, to join me and manage the house. Then I had to liquidate my assets, since the cash had gone for doctors' bills. The house on Adams Boulevard was worth more than $200,000 but in desperation I sold it for $35,000 cash. The antique collection was auctioned off and the properties in New Hampshire, Oklahoma, and Redlands put up for sale. Then the government informed me I owed $120,000 in back income taxes!"

Breakdown

Busby Berkeley was at the very bottom. The mental anguish of the past year, the financial burdens, and the apparent collapse of his career now drove him to attempt suicide. "I remember going into the bathroom one morning, taking a razor blade, and slashing my throat and wrists. My houseboy must have heard me collapsing—he picked me up, carried me to the bedroom, and bandaged me by tearing up a bedsheet.

"He called the police, and I was taken to the hospital, where I was treated. Afterward, I was taken to the psychopathic ward of the Los Angeles General Hospital. It was a nightmare. I was thrown in with a lot of dirty, disheveled, bedraggled characters. They were so short of space that my cot was placed in the corridor, where these horrible creatures passed me day and night. One morning I heard an orderly tell someone that a man had just died in a nearby cell. They wheeled him out and wheeled me in, saying, 'Sorry, Mac, it's the only empty cell. You'll get used to it,' clanging the iron door shut. I knew that if I wasn't already mad, I soon would be. My wife was allowed to visit me just once a week. She gave me something to cling to—the hope of getting out."

Berkeley had to plead his case before a judge in order to be released. "The judge moved down the hall from cell to cell, and I had to stand in the entrance to my cell and present a convincing argument. I told him I realized I had done wrong in trying to take my life, but explained as best I could the circumstances that had led to it. I said I felt sufficiently recovered to leave and that I would like to go to a private sanitarium to regain my health. He agreed to this.

"When I reached the sanitarium I had to put up another convincing argument in order to avoid shock treatments and medication. I just wanted to rest. After six weeks I was given a clean bill of health. My weight had gone from 170 pounds to 107, but I knew I was all right, and I prayed to God for strength. I was determined to get back into films."

Life took on some semblance of order as Berkeley moved back into a small house with his wife and his houseboy. His mother's estate was settled in probate court. After all the fees, charges, costs, debts, and back taxes had been paid he was left with exactly seven hundred and fifty dollars. "After all I had been through, I was grateful to get that."

Comeback

It was 1948 before Busby Berkeley resumed his career in films. A lucky call to a friend, George Amy at Warner's, helped to end the long period of illness, depression, and unemployment. Amy had been closely associated with Berkeley as his film cutter. Now he was with director Michael Curtiz, who had his own production company at Warner's lot. Amy enthusiastically invited Berkeley to join him for lunch and the two spent a pleasant time reminiscing. Berkeley went to visit Jack Warner's office, saying that he had an appointment. Since Berkeley was well known, the secretary thought she had neglected to note the appointment. Warner was out of his office but eventually came back, greeted Berkeley affably, and listened as Busby explained the circumstances when he had rashly requested his release. Warner seemed genuinely sorry and offered Berkeley a job working with Michael Curtiz on Doris Day's film, *Romance on the High Seas*, to advise and supervise musical numbers. Thus Warner gave Berkeley the comeback opportunity he so badly needed.

Romance on the High Seas launched Doris Day on her Hollywood career and also proved that Busby Berkeley was as capable and authoritative as before. When Arthur Freed lined up his production of *Take Me Out to the Ball Game*, Berkeley was chosen as director. Long famous as a lyricist, Freed had begun his distinguished series of film musicals, directed by Berkeley, in 1940 with *Babes in Arms*.

But the decision did not rest entirely with Arthur Freed—Berkeley would have to pass muster with the mighty mogul, Louis B. Mayer. "Arthur and I went in to see Mayer, who liked to play God. I told Mayer I believed myself to be as good a director now as I had been in the past. He took a long look at me and asked what made me think so. I said, 'Because from all my troubles I've learned something.' This intrigued him. I told him I had learned a saying—'I have traveled a long way over sea and sod, and I have found nothing as small as me, and nothing as great as God.' Mayer was a pious man and this, coming from me, rather shook him. He sat silent for a while and then said quietly, 'God bless you, Buzz, God bless you,' then, turning to Arthur said, 'Buzz will direct *Take Me Out to the Ball Game.*' "

Berkeley justified Freed's and Mayer's faith in him. The film was a box-office winner. The Hollywood adage that a man is only as good as his last picture began to operate in Berkeley's favor, and he was assigned to direct *Annie Get Your Gun*, with Judy Garland. But this turned out to be more bad luck for Berkeley. "I had gotten along beautifully with Judy in the past; as a youngster she had been very easy to handle and totally cooperative. But something had happened in the years since we had worked together. She had great emotional and drinking problems then and as it was later revealed, problems with drugs. She could never be relied upon to show up for work. Sometimes she would be bright and peppy, other times tired and sleepy. The situation became impossible, the filming was crippled, costs soared. I advised Freed to get Betty Hutton to replace Judy, but neither he nor the others would take this suggestion. The stress and strain began to tell on my health. I wasn't going to go through that hell again, so I asked Freed to release me from the picture. While this was going on, Louis B. Mayer resigned and Doré Schary became production chief. Both Schary and Freed tried to get me to stay on, but I explained, 'Judy is very sick, and the production has become impossible. I can't afford to let it undermine my health.' They let me go, and hired Charles Walters in my place. Four days later production was halted when Judy threw a tantrum on the set and collapsed. With that, she was taken off the project. A while later, they signed Betty Hutton to play Annie, and George Sidney to direct. It was a bitter disappointment for me."

Setback

Take Me Out to the Ball Game, for which Berkeley won the film industry Exhibitor's Laurel Award for 1949, would be his last effort as a director, despite the picture's great success. Berkeley, however, did get assignments as the director of musical segments, beginning with *Two Weeks With Love*.

The early 1950's in Hollywood were difficult because of television's impact. The number of films in production dropped drastically—major studios cut back their payrolls and dumped most of their contracted actors. Times were hard even for those who were well entrenched in the industry. Berkeley worked on half a dozen film musicals from 1951–1953, the last one a remake of *Rose Marie*. Although they all had interesting and entertaining Berkeley creations, the times were against him. In the battle with television, the musical was the chief casualty and the studios brought about their own stiffest competition with the release of their film libraries to the new medium.

The original movie musical was extinct. In the years to come, musicals would be few and far between, almost always film versions of Broadway. What had been feasible in the mid-thirties had become impossible by the mid-fifties. Film production costs had doubled and tripled and labor unions had prohibited long working hours. Audiences could also see light musical entertainment on television and the scope of television produc-

THE FILMS
OF
BUSBY
BERKELEY

WHOOPEE

The Indian Dance from one of the first of Berkeley's famous overhead shots—an early example of Busby's "hindsight."

The Indians regroup in what was soon to become the special Berkeley touch—close formation and perfect, fearless symmetry.

WHOOPEE

Produced by Samuel Goldwyn and Florenz
   Ziegfeld/1930
Directed by Thornton Freelan
Screenplay by Stuart Heiser
Based on the play *The Nervous Wreck* by Owen
   Davis
Photographed by Lee Garmes, Ray Renahan, and
   Gregg Toland
Songs: *Making Whoopee*
     Stetson
     My Baby Just Cares For Me
     A Girl Friend of a Boy Friend of Mine
       by Gus Kahn and Walter Donaldson

     I'll Still Belong to You
       by Edward Eliscu and Nacio Herb Brown

Dances staged by Busby Berkeley

Running time: 85 minutes

Cast: Henry Williams . . . . Eddie Cantor
      Sally Morgan . . . . Eleanor Hunt
      Wanenis . . . . Paul Gregory
      Sheriff Bob Wells . . . . John Rutherford
      Mary Custer . . . . Ethel Shutta
      Jerome Underwood . . . . . . Spencer Charters
      Black Eagle . . . . Chief Caupolican
      Chester Underwood . . . . Albert Hackett
      Andy McNabb . . . . Will E. Philbrick
      Judd Morgan . . . . Walter Law
      Harriett Underwood . . . . Marilyn Morgan

Whoopee is based on *The Nervous Wreck*, a story whose title gives a clue to the content. Cantor plays a hypochondriac who soothes his body with pills and potions, and airs his injured and worried soul in periodic outbursts of song. The setting, an elaborate dude ranch in Arizona complete with cowboys, Indians, and a bevy of gorgeous girls, provides a vivid Western background for the color cameras.

In this first of his films, Busby Berkeley's genius for staging is notable in the scintillating procession of equestrian beauties who ride down a Western trail in the manner of Lady Godiva. His overhead shot of dancing Indian maidens is an innovation which drew immediate approval and a device which was soon to become one of his trademarks.

Eddie Cantor, one of Broadway's brightest lights, made his screen debut in 1926 in *Kid Boots* but the picture made little impression. Although he appeared in two subsequent films, his Hollywood career didn't gain real momentum until he made *Whoopee*. Born in poverty on the Lower East Side of New York in 1892, Cantor became an entertainer while still a child. In 1916 he was put under contract by Florenz Ziegfeld, and over the years gradually became one of the greatest stars of the immortal Ziegfeld Follies. With the success of *Whoopee* he moved to Hollywood where he remained for the rest of his life.

Whoopee was a film version of the Broadway musical of the same name, produced by Ziegfeld and starring Cantor, which opened in December 1928, and enjoyed a long run. It seemed to be the best vehicle for Cantor's transition from stage to screen star. He and Ziegfeld discussed the property with Samuel Goldwyn, who was also looking for a story to be filmed in color. *Whoopee* would be Goldwyn's first musical and he knew he would need particular help with choreography and staging to support the box office, where musicals were slow. Conferring with Cantor and Ziegfeld, it was agreed that the best man for the job was Busby Berkeley.

The score for Broadway's *Whoopee* sported songs by lyricist Gus Kahn and composer Walter Donaldson. For the screen adaptation, Goldwyn and Ziegfeld decided to drop all but "Making Whoopee," one of Cantor's biggest hits, and induced Kahn and Donaldson to create three new songs. This would become standard practice in the 1930's and 1940's whenever films were made from stage musicals. Such changes would puzzle a public largely unaware that studios owned or were affiliated with music publishing houses and that royalties from songs written especially for films were paid to the studios.

Color had been used throughout the 1920's, principally for special sequences in films. Warner's, elated with their success in sound, launched into a series of color films, beginning with two musicals—*On With the Show* and *The Gold Diggers of Broadway*. The color boom, like the musical boom itself, would slow down with public disenchantment. The process was still a two-color one—more pleasing to the eye than faithful to the illusion. Later, when the third primary color was added to the process, Technicolor moved toward greater fidelity, although the cost kept it from being a viable commodity until the late '30's. But *Whoopee*, with sharper images and less grain than previous color pictures, received a boost at the box office.

Berkeley rehearsing the chorus for the "Stetson" number. Tom Mix, please take note: the white hats are the *good* guys.

PALMY DAYS

A Samuel Goldwyn Production/1931
Directed by Edward Sutherland
Screenplay by Keene Thompson
Based on a story by Eddie Cantor, Morris Ryskind,
   and David Freeman
Photographed by Gregg Toland
Songs: *My Baby Says Yes, Yes*
     There's Nothing Too Good for My Baby
       by Eddie Cantor, Benny Davis, and
        Harry Akst
     Bend Down Sister
       by Ballard MacDonald and Con Conrad

Dances directed by Busby Berkeley
Running time: 80 minutes
Cast: Eddie Simpson .... Eddie Cantor
      Miss Martin .... Charlotte Greenwood
      A. B. Clark .... Spencer Charters
      Joan Clark .... Barbara Weeks
      Joe the Frog .... George Raft
      Yolando .... Charles B. Middleton
      Stephen Clayton .... Paul Page
      Plug Moynihan .... Harry Woods

In *Palmy Days*, Eddie Cantor is the unwitting assistant to a gang of phony fortune tellers and spiritualists who plan to rob one of their gullible patrons, the millionaire owner of a bakery. By the usual string of accidents, Cantor is mistaken for an efficiency expert and given the run of the huge bakery and restaurant that also happen to employ a large number of girls—all of them pretty, shapely, and capable of formation dancing.

The gang, led by young George Raft, suspects that Cantor may double-cross them and threatens to kill him unless he hands over the employees' twenty-five-thousand-dollar Christmas bonus. In the last reel, Cantor, outwitting the crooks, leads them on a wildly comic chase. Having convinced the boss of his honesty he gets grabbed for the altar by Charlotte Greenwood, the energetic Amazon who runs the bakery's gymnasium and who has a fixation on getting Cantor into shape.

Cantor's big comedy scene in *Palmy Days* occurs during the chase. Finding himself in the ladies' locker room disguised as a girl, he is forced first to strip for a shower and then to go into the pool with the girls. Cantor, who appears in almost every frame of film, was expert at this type of comedy.

Palmy Days was produced on a smaller scale than most of Cantor's other pictures for Goldwyn, but "My Baby Says Yes, Yes" became a part of his permanent repertoire of songs. Busby Berkeley is clearly on hand, prismatically photographing the gorgeous Goldwyn girls. Overhead camera shots—soon to become known as Berkeley top-shots—and his distinctive use of lighting proved that there was room in movie musicals for a man with new ideas and vision.

Eddie Cantor (center), in classic comedy disguise, looks curiously like Jack Lemmon in *Some Like It Hot*, decades later. Charlotte Greenwood (right), looking doubtful, adds a few finishing touches.

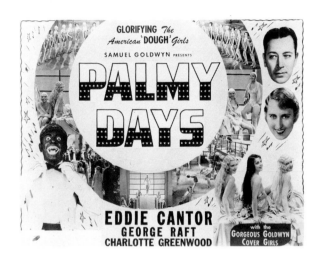

Thirty-three Berkeley beauties stay trim in an example of Berkeley's unexpected settings for production numbers—this time a gymnasium. There's Betty Grable at age sixteen (2nd row, 3rd from right). Can you find Virginia Grey, Lucille Ball, and Virginia Bruce?

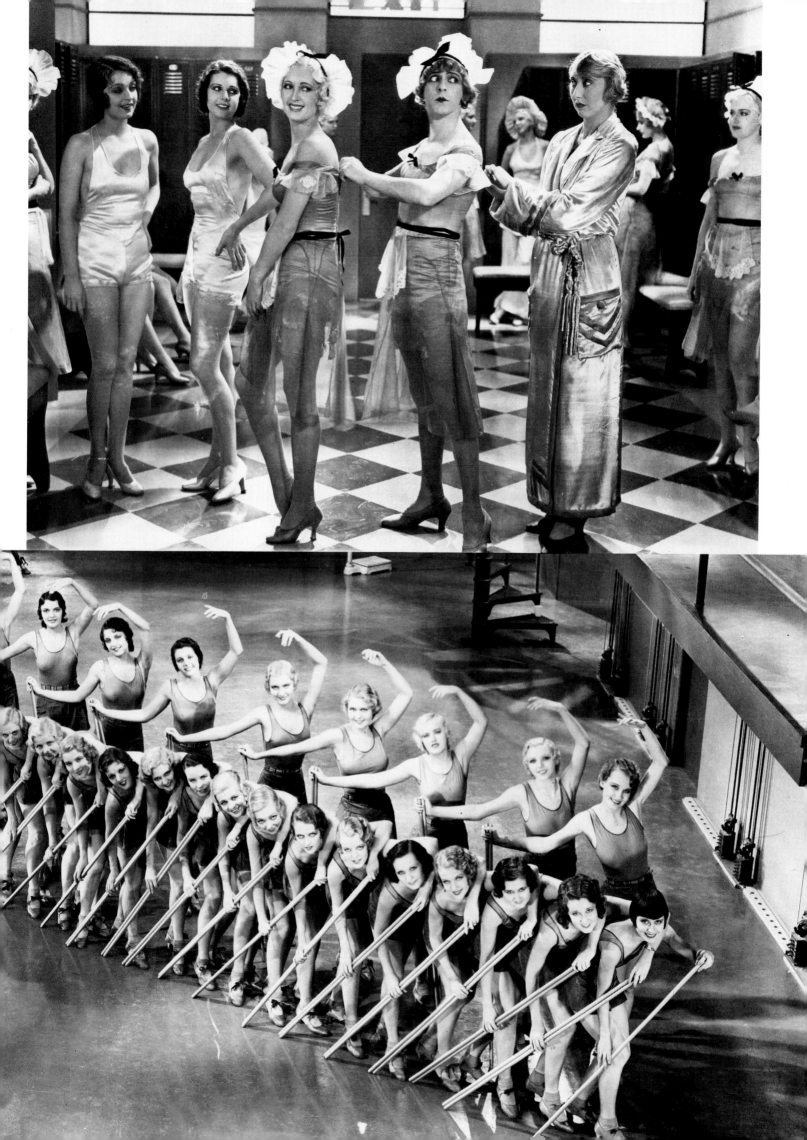

FLYING HIGH

An MGM Picture/1931
Directed by Charles Riesner
Screenplay by A. P. Younger
Based on the play by Buddy DeSylva, Lew Brown,
   and Ray Henderson
Dances directed by Busby Berkeley
Photographed by Merritt B. Gerstad
Songs by Jimmy McHugh and Dorothy Fields
Running time: 78 minutes
Cast: Rusty .... Bert Lahr
   Pansy .... Charlotte Greenwood
   Sport...................... Pat O'Brien
   Eileen .... Kathryn Crawford
   Dr. Brown .... Charles Winninger
   Mrs. Smith .... Hedda Hopper
   Mr. Smith .... Guy Kibbee

Flying High opened on Broadway in the spring of 1930. Produced by master showman George White, with book, lyrics, and music by the successful team of Buddy DeSylva, Lew Brown, and Ray Henderson, it enjoyed a healthy run and was quickly acquired by MGM for the screen. Unfortunately, by the time it was released as a film in December 1937, the public enthusiasm for movie musicals had virtually disappeared.

In *Flying High*, MGM did almost nothing to improve upon generally unimaginative handling of musicals on the screen. The producers dropped all but the title song and commissioned four new ones from composer Jimmy McHugh and lyricist Dorothy Fields. McHugh and Fields had written several highly successful tunes together, but in this instance they were unable to produce anything that would live beyond the picture.

Flying High introduced Bert Lahr to film audi-

Bert Lahr makes his Hollywood debut in this film version of a Broadway success.

ences. In making the film, Lahr, a sensitive and rather pessimistic man, came into contact with two of Hollywood's legendary figures—the dynamic young producer Irving Thalberg and the quiet tycoon Louis B. Mayer. Lahr was as amazed at Thalberg's good manners—a veteran vaudevillian, Lahr was not used to politeness—as he was appalled by Mayer's business dealings.

For Busby Berkeley, this film was a job with only two dance routines to stage. He used a chorus of forty girls and sixteen boys to back up two of the songs, planning dance routines cinematically and deploying the dancers in formations rather than having them merely dance steps. The ensembles were neatly worked out by Berkeley with the cameras up close enough to get a good look at the pretty girls.

Berkeley leaves no rhinestone unturned to bring the most decorative costume and set treatment to the screen. (Note the Art Deco and military motif that will appear again and again.)

NIGHT WORLD

A Universal Production/1932
Directed by Hobart Henley
Screenplay by Richard Schayer
Based on a story by P. J. Wolfson and Allen Rivkin
Dances staged by Busby Berkeley
Photographed by Merritt Gerstad
Musical score by Alfred Newman
Running time: 60 minutes

Cast:
Michael Rand	Lew Ayres
Ruth Taylor	Mae Clarke
Happy MacDonald	Boris Karloff
Mrs. "Mac"	Dorothy Revier
Klauss	Russell Hopton
Tommy	Bert Roach
Edith Blair	Dorothy Peterson
Clarence	Paisley Noon
Mrs. Rand	Hedda Hopper
Doorman	Clarence Muse
Ed Powell	George Raft
Policeman	Robert Emmet O'Connor

Night World made little impression upon the critics and audiences of 1932 and quickly passed into film limbo, not even to be redeemed by television since its scant running time of sixty minutes made it an awkward package.

The film takes place in a New York nightclub during the course of an evening. An alcoholic young patron (Ayres) finds solace in the company of a soft-hearted chorus girl (Clarke), while the club owner's wife carries on an affair with the club's dance director. Intertwined in the events are various characters—a pair of racketeers who are caught and rubbed-out by a policeman, a black floorman (Muse), and a platoon of chorus girls quipping about this and that.

The most interesting aspect of Night World is the casting. In 1930, Lew Ayres had made a great impression in All Quiet on the Western Front, but only twenty-three, he had yet to find an image. Mae Clarke, who gained a measure of fame in Public Enemy when James Cagney pushed a grapefruit in her face, still had no lasting career as a screen star. Hedda Hopper was making a consistent living as an actress, and Night World was one of her many appearances. Her subsequent notoriety as a journalist was still a few years away. The young man with the fixed, enigmatic expression and slick black hair, George Raft, was well known as a topnotch dancer but his bit in Night World did little to advance his career. His portrayal of a coin-flipping hood that same year in Scarface was the factor that most influenced his later image. The appearance of Boris Karloff in one of his few sympathetic roles is of particular interest in this film. He had first appeared on film in 1919, and had been consistently employed in pictures thereafter. Night World was actually his sixty-ninth film, and post-dated Frankenstein and The Mummy.

For Busby Berkeley, Night World was a minor assignment. "I was called in to direct the cabaret dance sequences with the chorus girls. It wasn't much of a challenge, but at this point I needed work and it was a job."

BIRD OF PARADISE

An RKO Radio Production/1932
Produced by David O. Selznick
Directed by King Vidor
Screenplay by Wells Root, Leonard Praskins, and
  Wanda Tuchock
Based on the play by Richard Walton Tully
Photographed by Clyde De Vinna
Musical score by Max Steiner
Title song by Milia Rosa and Peter de Rose
Dances directed by Busby Berkeley
Running time: 80 minutes

Cast: Luana . . . . Dolores Del Rio
  Johnny . . . . Joel McCrea
  Mac . . . . John Halliday
  Chester . . . . Richard (Skeets) Gallagher
  Thornton . . . . Creighton Chaney
                        (Lon Chaney, Jr.)
  Hector . . . . Bert Roach
  The King . . . . Pului

Often referred to as the most beautiful woman ever to become a film actress, Dolores Del Rio, a newlywed twenty-year-old aristocrat, visited Hollywood for the first time in 1925 at the invitation of director Edwin Carewe, who had been a guest at her home in Mexico City. Her family was horrified at the prospect of her being associated with the theatrical profession. Her husband indulged his bride's fascination with films, thinking she would soon be bored with it—he could not have been more wrong.

Dolores Del Rio became the first Mexican actress to achieve stardom in films. She spent eighteen years in Hollywood and then returned to Mexico to become the first lady of the Mexican film industry.

Bird of Paradise is a lavish, exotic South Seas romance, and costing more than one million dollars, it was one of the most expensive pictures of its time. King Vidor, in his autobiography *A Tree Is a Tree*, confessed that he thought so little of the original play *Bird of Paradise* that he couldn't finish reading it. But David O. Selznick, then head of production at RKO Radio, was determined to have Dolores Del Rio and Joel McCrea in a South Seas romance, and he said to Vidor, "I don't care what story you use as long as we call it *Bird of Paradise* and Del Rio jumps into a flaming volcano at the finish." With that, Vidor and writer Wells Root took off for Hawaii and worked on location until they had concocted a suitable story. Much of the film was actually shot in the Hawaiian islands.

The plot centers around the savage superstitions of Polynesia, principally the taboo placed upon the love of a white man for a native girl. The man (McCrea), drawn to the alluring native girl (Del Rio) for obvious reasons, soon finds his feelings for her turning into deep attachment. Denied the right to court her, they find sanctuary on an island that is forbidden ground. The gods seem to be on the side of the natives who hope the lovers will be destroyed during the violent and spectacular eruption of a volcano. Rescued by her lover's friends, the girl finally capitulates to the customs of her people. Climbing the mountain, she sacrifices herself to the volcano to appease the gods.

Bird of Paradise represents another minor Berkeley commission, "but a very pleasant one. King Vidor asked me to direct the scenes involving the dancing of the natives, particularly the ceremonial dances. I was happy to do it, but at the same time my ears and eyes were open for bigger and better jobs." Berkeley was in the near future to be involved in three other films with Dolores Del Rio, all bigger and better jobs.

THE KID FROM SPAIN

A Samuel Goldwyn Production/1932
Directed by Leo McCarey
Screenplay by William Anthony McGuire, Bert
    Kalmar, and Harry Ruby
Photographed by Gregg Toland
Songs: *In the Moonlight*
        Look What You've Done
        What a Perfect Combination
            by Bert Kalmar and Harry Ruby

Dances directed by Busby Berkeley
Musical direction by Alfred Newman
Running time: 96 minutes

Cast: Eddie .... Eddie Cantor
       Rosalie .... Lyda Roberti
       Ricardo .... Robert Young
       Anita .... Ruth Hall
       Pancho .... John Miljan
       Alonzo Gomez .... Noah Beery
       Pedro .... J. Carroll Naish
       Crawford .... Robert Emmet O'Connor
       Jose .... Stanley Fields
       Gonzales .... Paul Porcasi
       Dalmores .... Julian Rivero
       Martha Oliver .... Theresa Maxwell Conover
       Dean .... Walter Walker
       Red .... Ben Hendricks
       Sidney Franklin .... Himself

The Goldwyn Girls form a human tortilla in a Spanish café.
Berkeley assembled sets worthy of the Grand Canyon,
calling them cafés and nightclubs. It was Hollywood—it
was Berkeley—and it worked.

On the strength of the public reaction to Eddie Cantor in *Whoopee* and *Palmy Days*, Samuel Goldwyn invested one million dollars, then a high figure for a film, in the budget of *The Kid From Spain*.

As the story opens, Cantor and his chum Robert Young are being expelled from college. Shortly thereafter, they become inadvertently involved in a bank robbery, and unable to prove their innocence, they flee across the Mexican border. In Mexico, Cantor is mistaken for a famous matador, Don Sebastian, and since he is being hounded by detectives he poses as the bullfighter.

Life in the *corrida* soon teaches Cantor that *el toro* is not his only adversary. Not only is the life of a matador fraught with professional jealousies but when Cantor helps a friend win the affections of a señorita he also manages to incur the wrath of a notorious Mexican outlaw. Of course, he is also expected to enter the bullring.

The comic highlight in *The Kid From Spain* is Cantor's bullfight scene. With the police on the sidelines waiting to nab him as a fugitive, Cantor faces a wild bull which has been substituted for the tame one. Sheer luck gives him a perfect kill, winning the admiration of the *aficionados,* the girl he fancies, and even the police.

The Goldwyn Girls, well displayed in *The Kid From Spain,* are again put through their impressive paces by Busby Berkeley. One number, performed in a swimming pool, has the girls going through intricate formations in the water. Later in the film, there is a dance routine in a Mexican café, which takes advantage of the local talent.

Eddie Cantor (left) in one of the blackface minstrel numbers that made his star rise over Broadway. He and Busby were chums from Berkeley's New York days.

The Goldwyn Girls preparing for a dip in a pool the size of the Indian Ocean. Notice the tantalizing suggestion of nudity behind the screens (right); there is always generous feminine enticement in Berkeley's films.

48/ The Kid from Spain

A Dip in the Pool. In those days, they died with their boots
on and swam with their pumps on. The chorus, a Berkeley
specialty, has some very special faces: Paulette Goddard,
Lucille Ball, Betty Grable, and the ubiquitous Virginia
Bruce.

The Kid from Spain /49

42ND STREET

A Warner Brothers Picture/1933
Produced by Darryl F. Zanuck
Directed by Lloyd Bacon
Screenplay by Rian James and James Seymour
Based on a story by Bradford Ropes
Photographed by Sol Polito
Songs: *42nd Street*
     Shuffle Off to Buffalo
     Young and Healthy
     You're Getting to Be a Habit With Me
      by Al Dubin and Harry Warren

Dances staged and directed by Busby Berkeley
Running time: 90 minutes

Cast: Julian Marsh . . . . Warner Baxter
       Dorothy Brock . . . . Bebe Daniels
       Pat Denning . . . . George Brent
       Lorraine Fleming . . . . Una Merkel
       Peggy Sawyer . . . . Ruby Keeler
       Abner Dillon . . . . Guy Kibbee
       Barry . . . . Ned Sparks
       Billy Lawler . . . . Dick Powell
       Ann . . . . Ginger Rogers
       MacElroy . . . . Allen Jenkins
       The Actor . . . . Henry B. Walthall
       Terry . . . . Edward J. Nugent
       Jerry . . . . Harry Akst
       Leading Man . . . . Clarence Nordstrom
       The Songwriters . . . . Al Dubin and
                          Harry Warren

In 1933, Warner's, spurred by their great break-through with talking pictures, had over-invested their capital in musical films and a string of pictures filmed in color. Public enthusiasm for both color and musicals had tapered off drastically. Darryl F. Zanuck, then executive production chief for Warner's, persuaded the company to produce a musical, *42nd Street*, that would have a strong story and a superior cast, together with a fresh score and well-photographed production numbers. The budget was set at four hundred thousand dollars. Mervyn LeRoy became ill just prior to production and the project was handed over to Lloyd Bacon, but LeRoy had convinced Zanuck that the one man to get for the dance direction was Busby Berkeley.

42nd Street is the backstage musical par excellence. The harried producer of a musical comedy is trying to make his show a hit but he is saddled with the difficulties of a prima donna star, who also happens to be having an affair with the show's backer. Just a few days before the Broadway opening, the star gets drunk and sprains her leg. With the success of the show in jeopardy, one of the girls in the chorus suggests that there is a "real little trouper" in the cast who could step in and play the lead. Ruby Keeler, as Peggy, does just that. She is the classic ingenue, who has never been in love and has yet to receive her first kiss. The producer drills her almost to the point of collapse in order to get a performance out of her:

> Sawyer, you listen to me and you listen hard.
> Two hundred people, two hundred jobs, two
> hundred thousand dollars, five weeks of grind

and blood and sweat depend upon you. It's the lives of all these people who've worked with you. You've got to go on and you've got to give, and give and give! They've got to like you, got to! You understand? You can't fall down, you can't. Because, your future's in it, my future, and everything all of us have is staked on you. All right now I'm through. But you keep your feet on the ground and your head on those shoulders of yours, and, Sawyer, you're going out a youngster, but you've got to come back a star!

The casting in *42nd Street* is especially effective. Warner Baxter had long been a respected actor, and Bebe Daniels, who began her film career in 1919, is perfect as the temperamental actress. Dick Powell, signed by Warner's one year previously, had been given small parts in three films, but it was his appearance in this film that would trigger years of starring in film musicals. Ruby Keeler made her movie debut in *42nd Street* and became the principal discovery of the picture. She would go on to make nine musical films for Warner's, seven of them with Dick Powell. By 1939 she had retired from films. The film was Ginger Rogers's thirteenth appearance in the two years she had been in Hollywood. Mervyn LeRoy, whom she was then dating, persuaded her to take the small part. He afterwards gave her a bigger part in his *Gold Diggers of 1933*, and within the year she was chosen to co-star with Fred Astaire in *Flying Down to Rio*. Character actors like Guy Kibbee and Allen Jenkins were players in what was virtually a stock company for the Warner musicals.

Also making brief appearances in *42nd Street* were the two men who wrote the songs for the picture, lyricist Al Dubin and composer Harry Warren, New Yorkers who had been drawn to Hollywood by the prospect of new musical horizons. Warren had done well on Broadway with such songs as "You're My Everything" and "Would You Like to Take a Walk?" and during the twenty-year heyday of the film musical, he would continue to supply songs for some sixty pictures. With the success of *42nd Street*, Warren and Dubin were signed to a seven-year contract by Warner's and became that studio's principal songwriters.

Busby Berkeley had been signed for this one film, but before it was completed he too was under contract to Warner's for seven years. "I got a call from Zanuck not long after I had started my rehearsals, asking me if I could explain what I was doing. He came to the set that evening with an entourage of executives and I prepared to show him what we had planned for the number 'Young and Healthy.' I staged this with three revolving platforms, and I explained to Zanuck that I couldn't show him exactly what he would see on the screen because I planned to shoot in cuts. I outlined the continuity for him and showed him my camera placements, then had Dick Powell and the boys and girls go through the number in sections. Zanuck and the others seemed very pleased with the performance and the staging I had planned; he turned to the executives who were with him and said, 'Give Berkeley whatever he wants in the way of sets, props, costumes. Anything he wants, he can have.' Zanuck had great foresight and initiative—he broke

Berkeley on the boom, setting up the historic *42nd Street* production number. Each building is manned to sway with the beat of the music as the entire set comes alive.

Enter Ruby Keeler. The young wife of Al Jolson makes her Hollywood debut in this film after being a Ziegfeld Follies favorite. Her talent lights up the screen, and in the many times they would work together, the combination of Keeler and Berkeley always would produce something very special.

new ground with this picture. His confidence in me made a vast difference to my career."

Berkeley uses Ruby Keeler to particular advantage in staging the film's title song. She first appears in close-up doing a tap routine, and as the camera pulls back we find she's dancing on the top of a taxi. The huge set depicts the intersection of Broadway and 42nd Street, with all its noise and bustle. What looks like the skyline of Manhattan suddenly bursts into motion as the buildings dance—Berkeley has arrayed his dancers on a giant staircase with each girl holding a board on which a building has been painted.

Perhaps the most interesting number in *42nd Street* is "Shuffle Off to Buffalo." It gave Berkeley more problems than anything else in the picture. "Since it was a honeymoon song, I had them build me·a Pullman train carriage, one that would split down the middle as I moved my camera into the interior. I was then stuck for an idea on what to do once I got inside. I sat for three days in front of that set, and then during a lunch break it came to me, and what you see on the screen—the action inside the Pullman—was staged that afternoon."

42nd Street became a landmark film. It turned the tide for movie musicals, and helped Warner's grow into a major studio introducing new, great talent. With its success, Busby Berkeley was assured continuous employment for years to come. The film received lavish praise, especially for its production numbers. Writing in the New York *Herald Express*, Jimmy Starr voiced what was almost a consensus of opinion: "*42nd Street* is a cinematic effort by which Busby Berkeley, and he alone, is responsible for the current return of celluloid musicals. The beauty and originality of his dances top anything yet shown on the screen."

A *meringue glacé* of gorgeous girls, served up by Berkeley. Embellishments are increasingly inventive and fantastic, with a public clamoring for his next confection.

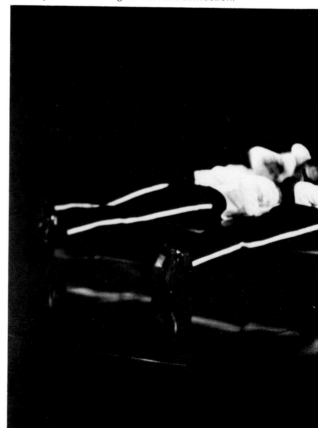

GOLD DIGGERS OF 1933

A Warner Brothers Picture
Directed by Mervyn LeRoy
Screenplay by Erwin Gelsey and James Seymour
Based on a play by Avery Hopgood
Photographed by Sol Polito
Songs: *I've Got to Sing a Torch Song*
   We're in the Money
   Pettin' in the Park
   Remember My Forgotten Man
   The Shadow Waltz
    by Al Dubin and Harry Warren

Numbers staged and directed by Busby Berkeley

Running time: 94 minutes

Cast:
J. Lawrence	Warren William
Carol	Joan Blondell
Trixie	Aline MacMahon
Polly	Ruby Keeler
Brad	Dick Powell
Peabody	Guy Kibbee
Barney	Ned Sparks
Fay	Ginger Rogers
Don	Clarence Nordstrom
Dance Director	Robert Agnew
Eddie	Tammany Young
Messenger Boy	Sterling Holloway
Clubman	Ferdinand Gottschalk

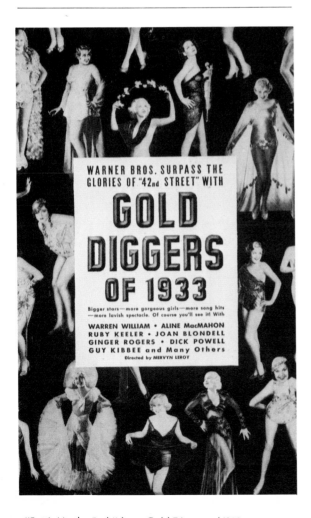

Setting up "Pettin' in the Park" from *Gold Diggers of 1933*. Again, Busby's titillating deployment of flesh and filmy underclothes shows up. (Notice the focus of the camera.)

Warner's lost no time in following up *42nd Street. The Gold Diggers of 1933* is even more elaborate, and has many more romantic complications. The plot has suave Warren William paired with Joan Blondell, middle-ager Guy Kibbee romancing Aline MacMahon, and Dick Powell and Ruby Keeler beaming at each other again. The three ladies are all in show business and share an apartment. Powell is a young blueblood whose family objects to his courting Ruby. William, his older brother, and Kibbee, the family lawyer, are sent in to break up the affair but instead fall in love with the two other girls.

In this movie Dick Powell is not only a renegade aristocrat, but also a budding songwriter determined to get into the theatre. He and the girls need financial backing for a show he has written and since he can't raise the funds from his obtuse family, the older brother and the lawyer are tricked into using their influence to get the necessary support. Once these plot devices are cleared away, the picture launches into some typical Berkeley flights of fancy, yet the fifteen thousand dollars mentioned as the budget for the show staged by Powell and his chum presents another Warner musical question best left unasked.

Director Mervyn LeRoy, who was unable to direct *42nd Street* due to illness, keeps the plot moving. LeRoy had directed his first film for Warner's in 1928 and was one of their busiest directors. He let Ginger Rogers open the picture wearing a gown of glittering coins and singing the theme song "We're in the Money." The optimistic lyrics, obviously designed to be a counterpoint to Depression blues, tell us "we've got a lot of what it takes to get along," although the line "you never see a headline about a breadline today" is possibly somewhat too optimistic. The song, a dandy opener for Ginger and the Gold Digger chorines, even has them break into Pig Latin, a fad of the time.

The Gold Diggers of 1933 is further testimony to the talents of Al Dubin and Harry Warren. With this second success the film musical was clearly becoming a new medium of expression, with the screen and camera expanding the interpretation and staging of musical numbers to a point that no theatre, whatever its budget or facilities, could possibly contain. Busby Berkeley had precisely the kind of fertile cinematic mind needed for the musical comedy extravaganzas.

The film has three big production numbers. "Pettin' in the Park" is amusing and slightly risqué with dozens of young men and their girl friends acting out the song's title. At one point a rainstorm drenches the participants and the girls run for cover. Changing their clothes in brightly lit rooms, behind drawn shades, the audience is treated to some enticing silhouettes. The number, bright and cheeky, is not as memorable as the two other Berkeley creations in the same film: "The Shadow Waltz" and "Remember My Forgotten Man."

Berkeley recalls that during the time he worked as a dance director in New York he would often visit the Palace, the famous vaudeville theatre, to look over the acts for inclusion in his own shows. "One afternoon I saw a girl come out on stage and

Berkeley Strikes Gold! The first of Berkeley's *Gold Digger* films strikes a successful formula of breezy comedy and elaborate production, just right for the escapist fare that people craved in the dreary 1930's. Three girls make it happen: from the left, Ruby Keeler, Joan Blondell, and Ginger Rogers, shown here "In the Money," one of the hit songs from the movie.

do a beautiful dance while playing a violin. I was very impressed and thought to myself I must do that sometime, but with more than one girl. When it came time to dream up ideas for this picture, I thought of the girl with the violin. But now I had no less than sixty girls at my disposal, so I ordered sixty white violins and a huge curving staircase for them to dance on. Once I had them go through the dance, it occurred to me that the number would be even more spectacular if the violins were all neon-lighted. The electricians fixed up each girl with wires and batteries and we were able to get some effective footage with the girls waltzing in the dark." "The Shadow Waltz," with its ever-appealing melody by Harry Warren, remains one of the all-time highlights in the Berkeley bag of tricks. The choice of a finale was influenced by the tenor of the times and conviction that the audience should be left with a definite inspiration.

"Remember My Forgotten Man" is a trenchant social comment, making a plea for the unemployed servicemen who had been hit hard by the Depression. One hundred and fifty extras were costumed as soldiers, and Berkeley had them march through a huge half-wheel contraption as Joan Blondell sang of the men who returned in triumph after fighting for their country, but who, fifteen years later, were reduced to standing in breadlines. As a moving plea for the unemployed, it undoubtedly met with passionate approval from the American Legion. Only a cynic could fail to be unmoved by its message or unimpressed by its brilliant staging.

Meticulous Berkeley, rehearsing the girls with violins for "The Shadow Waltz" number.

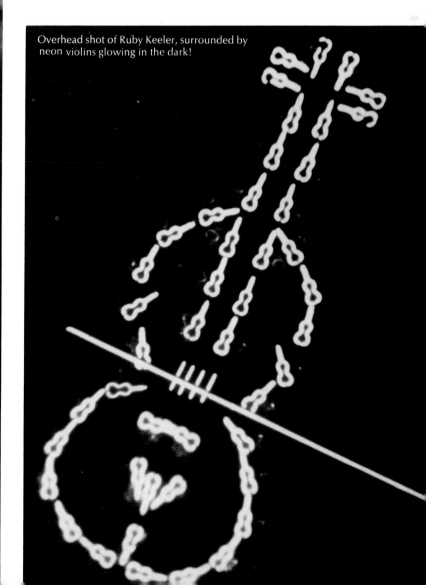

Overhead shot of Ruby Keeler, surrounded by neon violins glowing in the dark!

Joan Blondell (center) in one of Berkeley's unforgettable moments. The "Forgotten Man" sequence from *Gold Diggers of 1933* is a rarity—genuine spectacular Berkeley entertainment combined with a gritty, earnest emotional appeal—one of the earliest examples of social consciousness in a formula Hollywood musical.

SHE HAD TO SAY YES

A First National–Warner Brothers Production/1933
Directed by Busby Berkeley and George Amy
Screenplay by Rian James and Don Mullaly
Based on a story by John Francis Larkin
Photographed by Arthur Todd
Running time: 62 minutes

Cast: Florence . . . . Loretta Young
Maizee . . . . Winnie Lightner
Daniel . . . . Lyle Talbot
Tommy . . . . Regis Toomey
Luther Haines . . . . Hugh Herbert
Sol Glass . . . . Ferdinand Gottschalk
Birdie . . . . Susanne Kilborn
Mrs. Haines . . . . Helen Ware
Office Boy . . . . Harold Waldridge

Right from the beginning of his contract with Warner Brothers, Busby Berkeley made it clear that he wanted to direct films and not just invent musical sequences. Warner's was hesitant to grant his wish. They were not short of directors, but the impact of Berkeley's contribution to the success of their musicals obliged them to indulge him. For his first directing job, Warner's gave him a routine property, *She Had to Say Yes*, and assigned veteran film editor George Amy as co-director. "I learned a lot from George about the technical business of cutting and editing, which helped me greatly in building my own technique."

She Had to Say Yes stars Loretta Young in her last film for Warner's. She was only twenty years old, but had already appeared in forty films, starting with a bit part in First National's *Naughty But Nice* at the age of fourteen. Her role in this film was one of no less than nine, all in films released during 1933.

In this slight vehicle, Loretta plays a secretary in the garment business. With stiff competition and falling profits, the manager decides to use secretaries rather than professional "customer's girls" to entertain out-of-town buyers. Innocent Loretta is intrigued by the seemingly glamorous assignment and also sees it as an opportunity to pick up extra cash for her marriage fund. Fiancé Regis Toomey, a salesman for the same company, makes his objections known. Complications arise when Loretta entertains visiting buyer Lyle Talbot and the pair fall in love. A shady scheme to promote an important business merger causes Talbot to break off with her, but eventually he discovers she was not responsible for the tricky maneuver and all is well.

Looking back on *She Had to Say Yes*, Busby Berkeley recalls, "It was a routine picture but a pleasant one to do, and I learned not only that I could direct but that I liked it. Loretta, with those marvelous big gray eyes of hers, was a charming girl to work with. She had, and I imagine still has, a ladylike quality that is rather uncommon among actresses."

Berkeley proved he could successfully direct an entire film, and the musical numbers he devised and staged were footage for which he was still solely responsible. In his next film, *Footlight Parade*, Berkeley's musical numbers would constitute about one-third of the running time of the film. However, the director, Lloyd Bacon, would not be involved in Berkeley's sequences, and the same would be true of all the films to come.

She Had to Say Yes. The audience said *no!* Berkeley with no music, a nondescript property, and Loretta Young in the garment district! Could you ask for *less*? Here's Loretta, with Harold Waldridge (left) and Regis Toomey.

FOOTLIGHT PARADE

A Warner Brothers Production/1933
Directed by Lloyd Bacon
Screenplay by Manuel Seff and James Seymour
Photographed by George Barnes
Dances created and staged by Busby Berkeley
Musical Numbers: *By a Waterfall*
        Ah, the Moon Is Here
        Sitting on a Backyard Fence
           Music by Sammy Fain, lyrics by
           Irving Kahal

        Shanghai Lil
        Honeymoon Hotel
           Music by Harry Warren, lyrics
           by Al Dubin

Running time: 104 minutes

Cast:
Chester Kent	James Cagney
Nan	Joan Blondell
Bea	Ruby Keeler
Scotty	Dick Powell
Gould	Guy Kibbee
Mrs. Gould	Ruth Donnelly
Vivian	Claire Dodd
Bowers	Hugh Herbert
Francis	Frank McHugh
Frazer	Arthur Hohl
Thompson	Gordon Westcott
Apollinaris	Paul Porcasi

With the success of *42nd Street* and *The Gold Diggers of 1933*, Warner's had created a public demand for glittering musicals and at the same time handed themselves the task of keeping the production line rolling in high gear. *Footlight Parade* is third in the series and manages to be more impressive than its predecessors, thanks to a good script, nimble performances, Lloyd Bacon's crisp direction, and Busby Berkeley's ability to come up with yet more incredible cinematic-choreographic ideas.

Footlight Parade, a backstage musical, is without a doubt the best of its kind, although it paints no rosy picture of the theatrical world. The film also holds historical interest since it deals with a form of entertainment that flourished for several years and then died away—the production of "prologues," short stage musicals that preceded the showing of films in major houses. The opening shot of *Footlight Parade* has the neon news strip of the old Times Square Tower informing the world that talking films are in and that the silents are finished. James Cagney, who observes with disgust and disbelief, finds himself out of a job as producer of stage musicals because his callous employers (Kibbee and Hohl) are persuaded that talkies have killed-off live theatrical presentations. In response, Cagney comes up with an idea for a new venture—the production of pint-sized musicals to accompany first-run films.

Footlight Parade owes much of its pacing to the vitality of James Cagney. In Hollywood for only three years, Cagney had done thirteen films for Warner's, and this was his first screen venture as a

Ruby Keeler as "Shanghai Lil" with James Cagney (left).

CLIMAXING WARNER BROS.' GLITTERING PARADE OF MUSICALS!
Glorious "42nd Street"—magnificent "Gold Diggers"—actually surpassed by the master makers of musical films! . . . In this new show packed with surprising novelties! . . . Jimmy Cagney singing and dancing for the first time on the screen! Stupendous dance spectacles with hundreds of glorified beauties, staged UNDER WATER! New laughs and song-hits from Gold Diggers' famous stars . . . All directed and staged by the internationally famous creators of "42nd Street", Lloyd Bacon and Busby Berkeley. CAN YOU EVEN THINK OF MISSING IT?

"FOOTLIGHT PARADE"
JAMES CAGNEY • RUBY KEELER • DICK POWELL • JOAN BLONDELL
GUY KIBBEE • RUTH DONNELLY • FRANK McHUGH • HUGH HERBERT

singer and dancer. Although he had been a hoofer in vaudeville, this aspect of his talent had been played down in his film career to the disappointment of the many who were fascinated by his highly charged dancing style. Cagney did dance in a few minor films, but the musical highlights of a movie career devoted mainly to drama were his portrayal of George M. Cohan in *Yankee Doodle Dandy*, for which he won an Academy Award, and his role in *Footlight Parade*.

The first hour of *Footlight Parade* is concerned with preparations for the prologues and the behind-the-scenes machinations of the management and the talent. Then the film broadsides three spectacular productions in succession, each running a full reel of film (approximately eleven to twelve minutes).

The story provides another insight into the theatrical world of the early 1930's. Possibly more than most pictures of its kind, *Footlight Parade* presents show business as tough, exhausting, frantic, and occasionally furtive. James Cagney portrays a man so obsessed by the theatre that he neglects his wife, a decidedly vicious girl. His employers are a weak-spined duo who keep a double set of books enabling them to swindle profits. Cagney is further maneuvered by a spy on his staff who is stealing his ideas. As relief in this frenetic atmosphere, Joan Blondell shines as Cagney's soft-hearted but tartly tough secretary. In a well-written part, Blondell is both comic and appealing. Dick Powell, boyish and wholesome, wanders in as a nephew of the boss's wife and lands a job as a singer. He shows substance after a while and asks for a job with more responsibility, partly because he is smitten with Ruby Keeler, a mousy office girl who won't give him a tumble. Ruby, whose dowdiness is finally corrected, emerges not only attractive but also as a dancer. Frank McHugh, the harassed, worried, fretful dance director, seems to do nothing except rehearse squads of dancing girls day and night. Two of the film's songs—"Sitting on a Backyard Fence," and "Ah, the Moon Is Here"—are performed as part of the rehearsals.

Cagney, who must present his prologues to an influential impresario (Porcasi) before the opposition can present theirs, is determined not to be robbed of any more valuable production ideas. Closing rehearsals to visitors, he decrees that not only will the entire company be quarantined—eating, sleeping, and working in the building—but that all phone calls will be monitored.

In one incredible evening, the Cagney company races around New York by bus and stages sumptuous productions at three theatres in succession. First comes "Honeymoon Hotel," in style and character an extension of "Shuffle Off to Buffalo." Newlyweds Dick and Ruby check into a hotel that seems to be frequented only by young couples, where "every little Bridal Suite is Heaven." The

"By a Waterfall" set, with the hydraulic tower fountain at rest in the foreground. With lights under the water in the pool, the girls form a starburst on the surface. Shot from overhead.

The Hanging Gardens of Berkeley. A midsummer night's dream, lavish in every way except clothing. Berkeley at his most fanciful—the triumph of artifice over nature.

production has lovers leering at each other and parading the hotel corridors in nightgowns and pajamas. While the atmosphere smacks of a love camp, the fun is naive, innocuous, and merrily performed to a sprightly tune by Harry Warren with lyrics by Al Dubin, that leaves little doubt of intent—"Cupid is the night clerk, 'neath the skies above: he just loves his night work, we just love to love."

"By a Waterfall" is one of the most staggering pieces of musical fantasy ever realized on film. Running close to a quarter of an hour, the production is breathless—an elaborate aquacade of one hundred girls, led by Ruby Keeler, performing kaleidoscopic patterns in the water and climaxing in a huge human fountain.

Barely leaving time for the audience to catch its breath, Cagney and company scramble back into their buses and proceed to the last theatre and the "Shanghai Lil" sequence. Finding his leading man inebriated with stage fright, Cagney takes the part. In a Shanghai saloon, sailor Cagney sadly croons:

> I've covered every little highway,
> And I've been climbing every hill,
> I've been looking high,
> I've been looking low,
> Looking for my Shanghai Lil.

Eventually he finds her—Ruby with slant eyes and a jet black wig, and together in terpsichorean delight they tap up and down the bar. At the bugle call, Cagney and his sailor friends must return to their ship. Berkeley now has an opportunity to show his virtuosity with military drills as the sailors and their Chinese girl friends go through the paces doing configurations of the American eagle, the Stars and Stripes, and even Franklin Delano Roosevelt's face.

One segment of the "Shanghai Lil" number is a huge brawl with one hundred fifty sailors, marines, and assorted civilians flailing limbs and breaking furniture. Berkeley remembers his concern for the girls, who were intermingled through the saloon set. "Before the scene started I warned everyone about being careful with my girls. It was my habit to wear a whistle around my neck, and I would blow it whenever I wanted the action to stop. Near the end of the scene, with the action getting thick and frantic, I blew the whistle and yelled to the assistant director, 'Are the girls all right?' He walked around the debris and called back, 'Yes, all except for this one.' He picked up an unconscious girl and carried her off the set. She had stepped into a fist and was out cold, but she quickly rallied. I remember the incident so well because the girl, Lorena Layson, later became the wife of Louis B. Mayer."

Busby Berkeley describes the way the idea for "By a Waterfall" occurred to him. "It was at the premiere of *The Gold Diggers of 1933* at Grauman's Chinese Theatre on Hollywood Boulevard. Jack Warner and I were coming out of the theatre and Sid Grauman came up to me and said, 'Buzz, how the hell are you going to top "Shadow Waltz" and "My Forgotten Man"? What are you going to do for your next picture?' Something instantly came to my mind, something I hadn't thought of till that moment, and I told him, 'Sid, I can see a big waterfall

Ruby Triumphs. Here she is as top kitten in "Sitting on the Backyard Fence."

coming down through the rocks, with girls sliding down the rapids into a huge Ziegfeldian pool with twenty-four gold springboards and a gold fountain telescoping into the air. . . !' With that, Jack Warner interrupted, 'Sid, don't pay any attention to him, he's just blown his top.' We laughed and said good night. But on my way home I thought to myself, 'That's a pretty good idea—why not?' When it came time to devise things for *Footlight Parade* I mentioned it to Jack Warner, who blanched at the probable cost, but our pictures had been doing so well financially he had pretty well agreed to let me do whatever I wanted. So I designed my set and consulted with the art directors, the engineers, the carpenters, the electricians and told them what I wanted. The mountain wilderness and the pool covered almost an entire sound stage. The pool mea-

sured eighty feet by forty, and while the number was being shot we pumped twenty thousand gallons of water a minute over the falls and into the pool. I had them build me plate-glass corridors underneath the pool so I could light and shoot it from the bottom. People were constantly visiting the set to see if what they had heard was true. What with all the water pumps, the hydraulic lifts, and the dozens of workmen, someone said the set looked like the engine room of an ocean liner."

Busby Berkeley's main problem with this famous creation was finding the music. "I had this huge set built and I knew what I wanted to do with it, but I still didn't have a song. Harry Warren and Al Dubin were away on vacation, so I invited any composer who thought he had something to come and see me. I heard lots of melodies but not one I consid-

ered suitable. I wanted something particular, something special for a water ballet. I was getting frantic. One day a couple of young fellows came in. I had never seen or heard of them before, but I was eager to hear anything at that point. They weren't halfway through the song when I knew this was it— 'By a Waterfall.' The pianist was Sammy Fain and the singer was his lyricist, Irving Kahal. I was delighted, and so were they, because this was a big break for them and later they were among the busiest songwriters in Hollywood."

At the premiere of *Footlight Parade* in New York, the capacity audience cheered and gave "By a Waterfall" a standing ovation, some even throwing their programs into the air. In varying degree, the reaction has remained the same wherever and whenever the picture is shown.

ROMAN SCANDALS

A Samuel Goldwyn Production/1933
Directed by Frank Tuttle
Screenplay by George S. Kaufman, Robert Sherwood,
    and William Anthony McGuire
Photographed by Ray June and Gregg Toland
Songs: *Keep Young and Beautiful*
        Build a Little Home
        No More Love
        Rome Wasn't Built in a Day
        Put a Tax on Love
            by Al Dubin and Harry Warren

Numbers staged and directed by Busby Berkeley
Musical direction by Alfred Newman
Running time: 92 minutes
Cast: Eddie . . . . Eddie Cantor
         Olga . . . . Ruth Etting
         Princess Sylvia . . . . Gloria Stuart
         Josephus . . . . David Manners
         Empress Agrippa . . . . Verree Teasdale
         Emperor Valerius . . . . Edward Arnold
         Majordomo . . . . Alan Mowbray
         Manius . . . . Jack Rutherford
         A Slave Girl . . . . Grace Poggi

Roman Scandals is by far the most eye-appealing of the films Eddie Cantor made for Samuel Goldwyn. It fairly bursts with exotic hokum and vigorous low comedy against a background of Imperial Rome. It is also the sexiest of the movie musicals, with sets overrun by droves of pretty, scantily clad young ladies. For one slave-market sequence, Busby Berkeley persuaded a number of girls to appear completely nude. They agreed, provided the sequence was filmed at night on a closed set with their long blonde wigs as strategic covering.

Eddie Cantor, a wistful lad from West Rome, Oklahoma, is an ancient Rome buff. He accidentally finds evidence that the town's leading citizen is as crooked as the wicked Emperor Valerius, and daydreaming his way back to Roman times, imagines what he would do if he had the power. The plot structure of *Roman Scandals* resembles an adult, slightly lascivious version of *The Wizard of Oz*. One long sequence in a sumptuous bath of immense proportions showcases the elaborate set in a fully "Deco"dent style.

Harry Warren and Al Dubin supplied *Roman Scandals* with five excellent songs. The best of them, "Keep Young and Beautiful," is a lecture to the girls. "No More Love" is a haunting torch ballad by Ruth Etting, whose stormy life was later portrayed by Doris Day in *Love Me or Leave Me*. The melody perfectly suited her restrained style. The number starts quietly and slowly builds to a stunning plethora of girls, girls, girls. Torrid bits of dancing blend into the dramatic slave-market scene.

In the finale, a comic chariot race renders Cantor unconscious and returns him to Oklahoma.

Cantor's ebullient personality, the music, romance, comedy, costumes, dancing, and girls were welcomed by Depression-weary audiences of 1933 who for a short time also were allowed to escape their daily lives.

This was the last film Berkeley directed for Goldwyn. As Berkeley was under contract to Warner's, Goldwyn sued Warner's for Berkeley's services. A court case then ensued. The screenwriters, George S. Kaufman and Robert Sherwood, esteemed and legendary Broadway playwrights, stipulated that Eddie Cantor could not alter the story or dialogue. When Cantor made changes, they resigned and the result was another court case. Kaufman and Sherwood won and returned to New York.

Berkeley auditioned legions of girls to select the hundred or so the picture required, and recalls that he and Goldwyn agreed on their choices, with the exception of two girls Goldwyn didn't like. Berkeley, however, insisted on hiring them—Barbara Pepper (who became a popular character actress) and Lucille Ball.

Human Bondage à la Berkeley.
The girls are completely
nude under all that hair!

The rehearsal and final version of one of the elaborate production numbers with Eddie Cantor and more than a hundred showgirls.

WONDER BAR

A Warner Brothers—First National Picture/1934
Produced by Robert Lord
Directed by Lloyd Bacon
Screenplay by Earl Baldwin
Based on a play by Geza Herczeg, Karl Farkas, and
   Robert Katscher
Photographed by Sol Polito
Songs: *Wonder Bar*
        Why Do I Dream Those Dreams?
        Don't Say Goodnight
        Going to Heaven on a Mule
        Vive La France
        Tango Del Rio
         by Al Dubin and Harry Warren

Numbers created and directed by Busby Berkeley
Running time: 90 minutes
Cast: Al Wonder . . . . Al Jolson
      Liane . . . . Kay Francis
      Ynez . . . . Dolores Del Rio
      Harry . . . . Ricardo Cortez
      Tommy . . . . Dick Powell
      Simpson . . . . Guy Kibbee
      Mrs. Simpson . . . . Ruth Donnelly
      Pratt . . . . Hugh Herbert
      Mrs. Pratt . . . . Louise Fazenda
      Mitzi . . . . Fifi D'Orsay
      Claire . . . . Merna Kennedy
      Hal LeRoy . . . . Himself
      Richards . . . . Henry O'Neill
      Captain von Ferring . . . . Robert Barrat
      Mr. Renaud . . . . Henry Kolker

Wonder Bar. The stars: (from left) Dolores Del Rio, Dick Powell, Al Jolson, and Ricardo Cortez.

By now the moviegoer, even if he didn't bother to read the credits, could expect the big Warner musicals to contain fantastically staged dance numbers. The problem for Busby Berkeley was to keep up the standard he had set. *Wonder Bar* was ample evidence that his imagination was still in superb working order. There was a moment in *The Gold Diggers of 1933* when he tilted his camera at ninety degrees, with girls mirrored in a lake and pirouetting down either side of the screen. In *Wonder Bar* he topped that trick by building a huge octagon of mirrors projecting girls into infinity. As film historian Arthur Knight observes in his book, *The Liveliest Art*, "He was producing the purest combination of sound and vision that had so far come from an American studio."

Some reviewers of the time thought *Wonder Bar* topped its predecessors in entertainment value. It presents a strong cast, plus half a dozen musical numbers mixed with comedy, romance, drama, suspense, and even a bit of tragedy—the story structure is reminiscent of Grand Hotel. Despite the large doses of music, Lloyd Bacon managed to blend the various episodes and maintain coherence.

The action takes place in an internationally famous London nightclub owned and operated by Al Wonder, a celebrated entertainer. For Jolson, the role was perfectly cast. Dolores Del Rio, the club's featured dancer, is madly in love with dance partner Ricardo Cortez, who scorns and rejects her affections. Wealthy Kay Francis, magnetized by Cortez, gives him her enormously valuable jewels. Both Jolson and his singing band-leader, Dick Powell, are in love with Del Rio, but she cares nothing for them. Guy Kibbee and Hugh Herbert are a pair of small-town businessmen vacationing with their wives, who develop a yen for club hostesses Fifi D'Orsay and Merna Kennedy (then the current Mrs.

Busby Berkeley). A German officer, Robert Barrat, spends one last glamorous night at the Wonder Bar before killing himself. Del Rio stabs Cortez when she realizes he will desert her for Kay Francis. Del Rio later responds to Powell's amorous interest, and the gallant Jolson steps aside so as not to interfere with their happiness.

Musically, *Wonder Bar* is a grand slam, with the singing of both Jolson and Powell, in addition to the Latin dancing of Del Rio and Cortez. Berkeley is spectacular with tremendously imaginative variations on the songs "Going to Heaven on a Mule," and "Don't Say Goodnight." Now outdated, "Going to Heaven on a Mule" deals with an old Southern field hand who is so attached to his mule that when he dies he takes the beast to heaven with him. Jolson, in his famous black face, passes St. Peter's gate with his beloved mule and enters a heavenly world of Berkeley fantasy, admirable in scope and execution, in which over two hundred boys and girls play black angels.

"Don't Say Goodnight" remains a stunning visual experience. First sung by Dick Powell, then danced by Del Rio and Cortez, the number continues into fantasy. "I had them build me sixty tall white movable columns, to move against a black background. The columns were on separate tracks, independent of each other and all controlled electrically. I had a hundred dancers dance with the columns. Then they all disappeared and in their place was a huge forest of silver trees with a white reindeer running around. To get the effect I wanted, I built an octagon of mirrors—each twenty-eight feet high and twelve feet wide—and inside this octad a revolving platform twenty-four feet in diameter. When I was drawing up my plans for this, everyone at the studio thought I had lost my mind. Even Sol Polito, one of the best cameramen I ever worked with couldn't figure out how I was going to photograph a production from the inside without the camera being seen. Actually, when I figured it out in my office using eight little compacts—the kind girls carry in their handbags—I discovered there was a way of moving at the center of the mirrors without being reflected."

Berkeley's octagon of mirrors is another example of his wild yet practical imagination. With reflections stretching into infinity, he makes his hundred dancers seem like thousands. *Wonder Bar* further proves that Warner's had a bona fide genius on their payroll.

The "Tango del Rio," riding the crest of the Valentino tango wave, with Dolores Del Rio and Ricardo Cortez.

The spectacular "Don't Say Goodnight" production, a
technical triumph of Berkeley's career. He did it with an
octagon of mirrors, shooting from above and at angles.
The infinite reflections make a hundred dancers look like
thousands.

FASHIONS OF 1934

A Warner Brothers—First National Picture
Produced by Henry Blanke
Directed by William Dieterle
Screenplay by F. Hugh Herbert and Carl Erickson
Based on a story by Harry Collins and Warren Duff
Photographed by William Rees
Songs: *Spin a Little Web of Dreams*
      Broken Melody
         by Irving Kahal and Sammy Fain

Numbers created and directed by Busby Berkeley
Running time: 80 minutes
Cast: Sherwood Nash .... William Powell
      Lynn .... Bette Davis
      Snap .... Frank McHugh
      The Duchess .... Verree Teasdale
      Baroque .... Reginald Owen
      Duryea .... Henry O'Neill
      Jimmy .... Phillip Reed
      Joe Ward .... Hugh Herbert
      Harry .... Gordon Westcott
      Glenda .... Dorothy Burgess
      Glass .... Etienne Giradot
      Feldman .... William Burgess
      Caponelli .... George Humbert

"Venus with her Galley Slaves" replete with ostrich feather oars. Berkeley's lavish use of feathers very nearly put the ostrich on the endangered species list.

Any film entitled *Fashions of 1934* was bound to date quickly, yet it is more interesting now than at the time it was made. Most films produced during the assembly-line years of the Hollywood studios were, like the fashions themselves, designed for oblivion. However, *Fashions of 1934* contains a sumptuous Busby Berkeley creation that by rights should be extracted and preserved.

It is a sprightly picture with an original and different story line on which to hang musical numbers. William Powell, ever the Dapper Dan, is a fashion swindler—a slick, unscrupulous manipulator of ideas stolen from famous couturiers. He uses theatrical methods to present the bootlegged designs and his partner in crime, his secretary, Bette Davis, often poses as a fashion model. Photographic assistant, Frank McHugh, keeps a miniature camera in the head of his cane. The three accomplices arrive in Paris where Powell's agents had been unsuccessful. They encounter a struggling young songwriter, Philip Reed, a California feather merchant, Hugh Herbert, desperately trying to persuade the couturiers to use more feathers in their fashions, and an old girl friend, Verree Teasdale, palming herself off as a Russian duchess. Powell spots a beautiful opportunity: his old girl friend is now attached to the leading couturier, Reginald Owen, whose designs he is after. Using the knowledge of her true identity, Powell inveigles the girl into showing him the couturier's newest creations. When they are caught, Powell, threatened with arrest, tells all. Owen decides to overlook the truth of his inamorata's past and suggests to Powell that they combine forces to stage a legitimate fashion extravaganza utilizing the young songwriter's music, Hugh Herbert's feathers, Powell's theatrical talents, and his own newest designs. The final show, an open sesame to Busby Berkeley's imagination, is a smash hit and leaves Powell considering an honest future.

The Berkeley finale of *Fashions* is a pageant of ostrich plumes with fifty girls forming a Hall of Human Harps, a Web of Dreams, and Venus with her Galley Slaves. Clad only in feathers, several curvaceous damsels become live decorations on huge harps. Fan-carrying female forms compose a sixty-foot-long galleon. A magnificent spider web of girls is photographed from overhead. Had anything like this actually occurred in any Paris salon, the couturiers need never have worried about fashion trends.

"The Hall of Human Harps." This mind-boggling spectacle prompted a now-famous article by an outraged mother entitled "I Don't Want My Daughter Growing Up to Be a Human Harp."

DAMES

A Warner Brothers Picture/1934
Directed by Ray Enright
Screenplay by Delmer Daves
Based on a story by Robert Lord and Delmer Daves
Photographed by Sid Hickox and George Barnes
Songs: *Dames*
I Only Have Eyes for You
The Girl at the Ironing Board
by Al Dubin and Harry Warren

*When You Were a Smile on Your Mother's
Lips and a Twinkle in Your Daddy's Eye*
by Irving Kahal and Sammy Fain

Try to See It My Way
by Mort Dixon and Allie Wrubel

Numbers created and directed by Busby Berkeley
Running time: 90 minutes
Cast: Mabel .... Joan Blondell
Jimmy .... Dick Powell
Barbara .... Ruby Keeler
Mathilda .... ZaSu Pitts
Horace .... Guy Kibbee
Ezra Ounce .... Hugh Herbert
Bugler .... Arthur Vinton
Songwriter .... Sammy Fain
Songwriter .... Phil Regan
Conductor .... Arthur Aylesworth
Maid .... Leila Bennett
Ellworthy .... Berton Churchill

Dames might well have been titled *The Gold Diggers of 1934*, since in concept and intent it amounted to the same thing. It also employed much

the same talent as the other big Warner musicals—Dick Powell and Ruby Keeler are again the young lovers, he an ambitious songwriter who has written a show that needs only a backer, and she his sympathetic romantic inspiration. Joan Blondell is the flip chorus girl who shakes down the ubiquitous Guy Kibbee for the backing money. The story line is even slighter in *Dames* than in some of the others, but it is enough to link the Busby Berkeley spectacles.

Of the five songs in *Dames*, the three written by Al Dubin and Harry Warren form the basis for the Berkeley routines. Mort Dixon and Allie Wrubel supplied the ballad "Try to See It My Way," which is reprised several times as a theme song, and Irving Kahal and Sammy Fain came up with the saucy number "When You Were a Smile on Your Mother's Lips and a Twinkle in Your Daddy's Eye." Fain appeared in the picture as a young songwriter.

"The Girl at the Ironing Board" is a novelty number; an unusual one for Berkeley since it calls for only one girl, Joan Blondell, a lovelorn laundress singing to the pajamas and the men's long underwear she irons. A forest of laundry begins to swing and sway to her song. Berkeley recalls, "At the end of the shooting Ray Enright came over and said, 'Now you see, Buzz, isn't it easier to work with just one girl?' I laughed and replied, 'Ray, look above you.' He did, and I pointed out some fifty men I had in the overhead racks manipulating strings attached to the underwear and the pajamas."

By far the most memorable item in *Dames* is the song and routine, "I Only Have Eyes for You." One of the best songs ever written for a film, it is sung by Powell and beautifully staged by Berkeley. Dick and Ruby meet in front of a movie theatre, then take a long subway ride during which they fall asleep. As Powell dreams—hordes of girls appear, all wearing Benda masks of Ruby so that an army of Keelers assaults the eye. Each girl, with a board on her back, bends over, and fitting the boards together, a gigantic jigsaw picture of Ruby's face appears.

The finale of *Dames* is another all-girl array for the title song. Here is fascinating rhythmic formation. A hundred girls in white blouses and black tights configurate, fragmenting here and there into abstract designs. Berkeley moves above for his celebrated overhead shot and the effect becomes a startlingly kaleidoscopic cacophony of geometric and floral mosaics.

The reviewers struggled to describe what had been achieved in *Dames*. The word "cinematerpsichorean" was coined to describe Berkeley's triumph, but its usage is defied by the number of letters it contains—inappropriate when the sheer number of girls in a sequence is considered.

In *Dames*, Berkeley's geometry surpasses Euclid. With precision formations that would send the Rockettes back to Kansas City, the chorus rivals the kaleidoscope and exceeds everything he has achieved up to this time. This jigsaw mask of Ruby Keeler is from "I Only Have Eyes for You."

"The Words Are in My Heart." Fifty-six white pianos and
fifty-six beautiful girls whirl in a military drill in waltz
time—an effect achieved by stagehands all in black,
carrying lightweight piano shells on their backs.

GOLD DIGGERS OF 1935

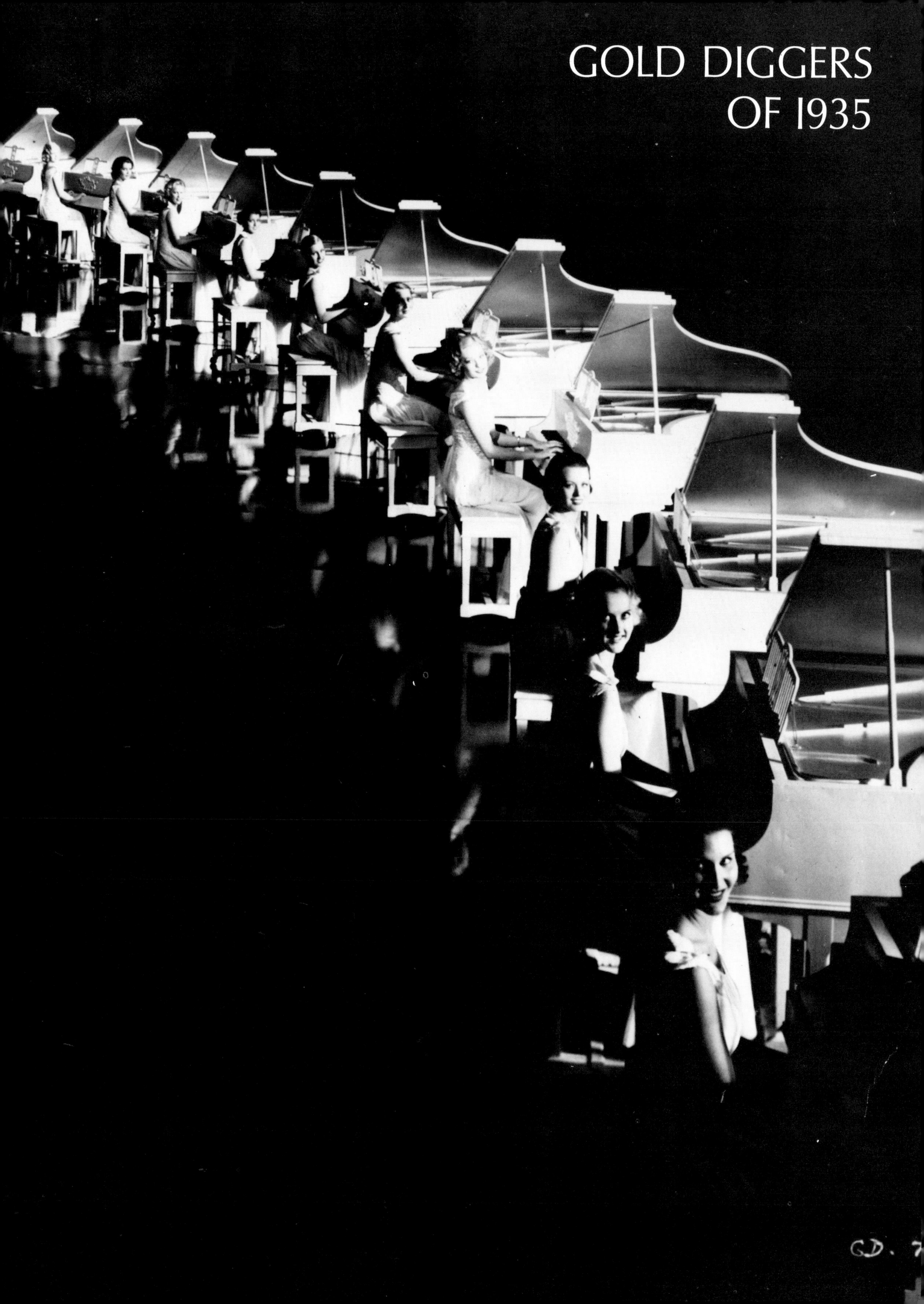

GOLD DIGGERS OF 1935

A First National Production for Warner Brothers /1935
Directed by Busby Berkeley
Screenplay by Manuel Seff and Peter Milne
Based on a story by Robert Lord and Peter Milne
Photographed by George Barnes
Dances created and staged by Busby Berkeley
Running time: 95 minutes.
Musical Numbers: *The Lullaby of Broadway*
                   The Words Are in My Heart
                   I'm Going Shopping with You

Music by Harry Warren, lyrics by Al Dubin

Cast:
Dick Curtis	Dick Powell
Nicoleff	Adolph Menjou
Ann Prentiss	Gloria Stuart
Mrs. Prentiss	Alice Brady
Betty Hawes	Glenda Farrell
Humbolt Prentiss	Frank McHugh
T. Mosley Thorpe	Hugh Herbert
Schultz	Joseph Cawthorne
Louis Lamson	Grant Mitchell
Arlene Davis	Dorothy Dare
Winny	Wini Shaw
Haggarty	Thomas Jackson

For his solo as a director, Warner's gave Busby Berkeley *The Gold Diggers of 1935*. They might have been a little more generous. The story is slight and the production is scaled along more economical lines than some of the previous Warner musicals. Although the score contains only three songs, Berkeley puts them to elaborate use, and one, "The Lullaby of Broadway," became a screen classic.

Warner's also saw fit to make *The Gold Diggers of 1935* a vehicle for Dick Powell, with Gloria Stuart taking third billing. Powell did well enough, but the vitality of Joan Blondell or Ruby Keeler might have helped him. The picture was loaded with a crew of solid character actors, all of whom were kept hopping under Berkeley's nimble direction. Everything learned from dance directing was applied to picture-making—the art of perpetual motion and movement.

The film is set in a swank New England summer hotel and opens with the staff preparing this rural Waldorf-Astoria for the arrival of the carriage trade. There are management lectures on the sharing of gratuities. Dick Powell, a medical student working as a clerk for the season, is engaged to the hostess, Dorothy Dare. Among the first guests to arrive is a parsimonious millionairess, Alice Brady, with her beautiful but shy daughter, Gloria Stuart, and her open-hearted but light-headed son, Frank McHugh. Rich but eccentric Hugh Herbert is Miss Brady's selection as a son-in-law, but his attentions are

Dick Powell and Wini Shaw, from the "Lullaby of Broadway" number.

Adolph Menjou, the suburban impresario, instructs a bouquet of Berkeley blondes.

Gloria Stuart and Dick Powell on the "Words Are in My Heart" set. From the looks on their faces, who dares to guess what words were in their hearts at the moment? Berkeley looks on.

confined to his snuffbox collection and his ambitions to write a book on the subject.

The annual charity show at the hotel is the occasion for hiring an eccentric Russian-accented impresario (Menjou). He, his assistant, and the hotel manager plot to split the entertainment budget. Powell is hired as an escort for the daughter and when they fall in love, Powell's former fiancée graciously lets him off the hook. She has her eye on bigger game—the son, since Mother has paid each of his former wives one hundred thousand dollars to annul their marriages. The venal tone of this film and the dickering of the impecunious to fleece the affluent could have amused during the Depression years.

Of the three songs in *The Gold Diggers of 1935*, only "I'm Going Shopping with You," is part of the story line, with Powell singing while escorting Gloria Stuart through a department-store shopping spree. The beautiful Gloria seems to delight in spending her mother's money. Powell lovingly croons, "The Words Are in My Heart," on a moonlight ride in a motorboat. The charity show is the foil for an elegant production number featuring fifty-six white evening-gowned young ladies, seated at fifty-six white baby-grand pianos.

The piano sequence is supremely Busby Berkeley, and typical of the cornucopia of ideas that abounded during those hectic years at Warner's. "I remember one day in New York I was watching an act at the Palace with four men playing grand pianos. I thought to myself then, 'Someday I'll do that with fifty pianos,' and when it came time to think of something for this song, the thought came to mind. I had them build me fifty-six grand-piano shells of fairly light construction so that I could move them in formation and perform a kind of military drill in waltz time. Harry Warren had written a waltz in the best Viennese hesitation style and that made it easier for me to devise a pattern of movement for the pianos."

Berkeley has been asked ever since how he managed to move fifty-six pianos like humans. The secret is simple. A little man under each piano wore black pants and followed black tape markings on the glossy black floor. An astute viewer is able to spot the human legs propelling the pianos, yet very few people have caught on to this particular Berkeley trick without it first having been explained. The piano ballet, while beautiful and impressive, is not appropriate for the finale of *The Gold Diggers of 1935*.

"The Lullaby of Broadway," a blockbuster, is Berkeley's favorite and was the most difficult to devise. Berkeley remembers, "Harry Warren came into my office one day while we were lining up the picture and he asked me to listen to something he had just written. It was immediately obvious that it was a great melody and I asked him if Al Dubin had come up with lyrics yet. It seems he hadn't, so I went right after him to get some. Al didn't seem to be able to think of anything, but after a fallow couple of weeks he suddenly hit on the idea of a song praising Broadway and a girl who sleeps by day and lives at night. Now it was up to me to stage it. I immediately knew how I wanted to handle the main

part of the number, but I was stuck for a way to open it. I had the reputation as a man who does things differently, and I couldn't just have a girl walking on stage singing the song. I racked my brains for several days. At one point Al Jolson burst into my office saying 'I've just heard the song Harry and Al have done for you, "The Lullaby of Broadway." It's marvelous, can I have it for my new picture?' I told him he couldn't, but he kept after me for about an hour and the only way I could get rid of him was to say, 'All right, Al, I'll tell you what. If I can't think of a way of starting this number in the next day, I'll let you have it.' He accepted this and left. Now I really had to sweat because if I couldn't think of an opening I'd have to give the song to Jolson, which I certainly didn't want to do. With that thought hanging over me, I eventually came up with an idea."

Busby Berkeley's "Lullaby of Broadway" is, like so many of his creations, almost a film within a film. It opens with singer Wini Shaw's face as a distant white dot on an otherwise black screen. As she sings the song, her face moves forward to become an isolated close-up on the black screen. The camera then swings around over her head focusing on her upturned face, which dissolves into an aerial view of Manhattan. A montage of New York hustle and bustle glimpses night owl Wini arriving at her tenement home as her neighbors prepare to go to work. The passage of day is indicated by the hands of a clock, and soon it is time for Dick Powell to call for Wini for another night of stepping out. We next find them the sole patrons of a gigantic nightclub. A pair of Latin dancers (Ramon and Rosita) enter and gracefully whirl to the strains of a muted version of the song, finishing on opposite sides of the floor. Each returns leading an army of tap dancers, who fill the screen like a slow tidal wave. Soon, one hundred boy and girl dancers in serried ranks are wildly dancing out the strains of "Lullaby of Broadway" as Berkeley photographs them in a torrent of camera angles. The sequence is breathtaking. As the routine finishes, Dick and Wini are drawn into the action for another round of gay abandon. Trying to escape the gaiety, Wini runs to a glass door opening onto a small balcony. She stumbles and falls from the skyscraper, screaming and twirling downward to her death. As the chorus sings in a hushed chant, Berkeley moves his camera through his New York montage, back to the girl's now-vacant room, then into the street. The glaring, glittering life of the Big City goes on. The opening sequence—an aerial view of Manhattan fades now, reversing into an overhead shot of Wini's face which fades into the distance as the last lines of the song are sung.

"The Lullaby of Broadway" is an incredible piece of film fantasy, which seldom fails to bring applause whenever it is shown.

The chorus shared top billing with every star in Berkeley's films. Here, a Lazy Susan of beauties from "Lullaby."

The finished sequence from the film.

Berkeley directs his stars in a test sequence from "Lullaby of Broadway"—Wini Shaw held in a bone-shattering embrace by the debonair Dick Powell.

BRIGHT LIGHTS

A Warner Brothers—First National Picture/1935
Directed by Busby Berkeley
Screenplay by Bert Kalmar and Harry Ruby
Adapted by Ben Markson and Benny Rubin
From a story by Lois Leeson
Photographed by Sid Wilcox
Songs: *She Was an Acrobat's Daughter*
       by Bert Kalmar and Harry Ruby

    Toddling Along with You
    You're an Eyeful of Heaven
       by Mort Dixon and Allie Wrubel

    Nobody Cares If I'm Blue
       by Grant Clark and Harry Akst

Running time: 82 minutes
Cast: Joe Wilson . . . . Joe E. Brown
       Fay Wilson . . . . Ann Dvorak
       Peggy . . . . Patricia Ellis
       Daniel Wheeler . . . . William Gargan
       Otto Schlemmer . . . . Joseph Cawthorn
       J. C. Anderson . . . . Henry O'Neill
       Wilbur . . . . Arthur Treacher
       Wellington . . . . Gordon Westcott
       Airport Attendant . . . . Joseph Crehan
       Detective . . . . William Demarest

Joe E. Brown, with his wide mouth, soulful eyes, and bashful manner, starred in a string of Warner comedies during the 1930's, all of them pleasing but none of them very memorable. *Bright Lights* was an ideal vehicle for him because in playing the part of a burlesque entertainer he could draw on his own considerable background in the same field. In reviewing the picture, one critic declared that it is an eighty-two-minute act by Joe E. Brown, with the comedian doing everything but taking the tickets.

The story is a familiar one, with extra punch in a scenario by songwriters Harry Ruby and Bert Kalmar, experienced vaudevillians. Brown appears as a low burlesque comic who makes good on Broadway, gets a swelled head as a result, loses his wife, and finally returns to vaudeville to reinstate his values. The film showcases Brown as he dances, sings, tumbles, does a drunk scene, tells corny old jokes, and recites the poem "Mousey," in addition to portraying a convincing and difficult character.

Bright Lights is a Busby Berkeley picture, and those chorines are undoubtedly cuter and shapelier than those who worked in real burlesque lines. The specialty of Brown's own career in vaudeville was tumbling, and this film revitalized his old act. Harry Ruby and Bert Kalmar contributed one song to the score of *Bright Lights*, a novelty number of the Flying Trapeze genre, "She Was an Acrobat's Daughter." Says Busby Berkeley, "This was one of the pleasantest assignments I ever had. We all admired Joe and it was fun all the way. For once I was sorry when the shooting was finished."

Joe E. Brown in a sequence from the film.

IN CALIENTE

A Warner Brothers—First National Picture/1935
Directed by Lloyd Bacon
Screenplay by Jerry Wald and Julius Epstein
Based on a story by Ralph Block and Warren Duff
Photographed by Sol Polito and George Barnes
Songs: *The Lady in Red*
    In Caliente
    To Call You My Own
       by Mort Dixon and Allie Wrubel

    Muchacha
       by Al Dubin and Harry Warren

Musical numbers directed by Busby Berkeley
Running time: 85 minutes
Cast: Rita Gomez .... Dolores Del Rio
      Larry MacArthur .... Pat O'Brien
      Jose Gomez .... Leo Carrillo
      Harold Brandon ..... Edward Everett Horton
      Clara .... Glenda Farrell
      Dance Team .... The DeMarcos
      Musical Quartet .... The Canova Family
      Singer .... Phil Regan
      The Girl .... Dorothy Dare
      Singer .... Wini Shaw
      Biggs .... Harry Holman
      Florist .... Herman Bing

Caliente is a Mexican resort town just across the border, and not far from San Diego. Famous for its horse racing, it has long been a popular spot with the Hollywood crowd

In Caliente stars Dolores Del Rio as a Mexican dancer whose act gets a severe pan from breezy magazine editor Pat O'Brien. Arranging to have him shanghaied in Caliente for revenge, they unwillingly fall in love. Hovering around is Edward Everett Hor-ton in his familiar role of faltering stooge, with Leo Carrillo as Dolores's handsome, dashing father.

The excellent musical numbers are the strength of *In Caliente.* Phil Regan handled the ballads, and Wini Shaw belted out "The Lady in Red." The De-Marcos performed elegant ballroom maneuvers which drew rounds of applause at the film's premiere. Judy Canova, then part of the Canova Family, made one of her first film appearances doing her crackerbarrel character. Lloyd Bacon's brisk direction kept the audience from dwelling too much on the story line, and Busby Berkeley had his usual fresh ideas on what to do with songs and dances.

In staging the "Muchacha" sequence, Berkeley had a hotel patio spring to life, turning it into a bandits' cave with Latin cowboys hopping around blazing campfires and doing rodeo routines. This and the other numbers in the picture lean heavily upon the fandango rhythms of the Caliente area. Part of the action involves a brawl in a café, with two hundred extras engaged in the melee, reminiscent of the brawl in the "Shanghai Lil" sequence in *Footlight Parade.* Berkeley says "I also used eight horses in this scene—they were supposed to crash through the doors and race through the café. I saw something go wrong during the fight scene so I whistled for the action to stop. The horses were standing on the stage near the set. My shrill whistle startled them and they stampeded. They galloped out of the studio, down the side streets, and out onto the back lot. It happened at lunch time, and as the horses galloped down the streets, people had to jump clear to keep from being knocked down. It took hours to find the horses and bring them back. As they raced past the commissary, one man looked up and said to another, 'There go Berkeley's horses. He must have dismissed 'em for lunch. Look at 'em go. He must be working their tails off.'"

Wini Shaw sings "The Lady in Red."

The "Muchacha" number. Above, from the barroom scene; below, an overall view of the set.

Dolores Del Rio in a rare quiet moment from *I Live for Love*, in which she plays a volatile South American actress. Here she is—lovely, fragile, difficult—with Everett Marshall.

I LIVE FOR LOVE

A Warner Brothers Production/1935
Produced by Bryan Foy
Directed by Busby Berkeley
Screenplay by Jerry Wald, Julius J. Epstein, and Robert Andrews
Photographed by George Barnes
Songs by Allie Wrubel and Mort Dixon
Running time: 64 minutes

Cast: Donna Alvarez . . . . Dolores Del Rio
Roger Kerry . . . . Everett Marshall
George Henderson . . . . Guy Kibbee
Jim McNamara . . . . Allen Jenkins
Howard Fabian . . . . Berton Churchill
Townsend C. Morgan . . . Hobart Cavanaugh
Rico Cesaro . . . . Don Alvarado
Street Musicians . . . . Shaw and Lee

Busby Berkeley was associated with three of the five films Dolores Del Rio made for Warner Brothers during 1934 and 1935—two as dance director and one, *I Live for Love*, as director. Berkeley proved himself a capable director, but the Warners handed him assignments only when there were no fantastic musical creations to be invented for their major attractions. The studio had the reputation for keeping a man's nose to his own particular grindstone.

I Live for Love is a musical, but with no elaborate productions. The story is a frothy, romantic comedy with the gorgeous Dolores playing a volatile, tempestuous South American actress whose fitful outbursts keep her producers on edge. Very well photographed by the talented George Barnes, Del Rio delivers a nicely spirited performance under Berkeley's always fluid direction, but the picture is hampered by the work of leading man, Everett Marshall. Marshall was a well-known radio and concert singer in the mid-thirties. Warner's gambled on his being able to make the transition to films, but his career was short-lived.

The plot of *I Live for Love* has Miss Del Rio trying to live up to the title by insisting that her current amour, an inferior actor and singer, become her co-star. The producer manages to ship him off on a Latin American tour so that he can bring in Marshall, a virile new singer, who is intended to captivate not only the public but the hot-blooded actress as well. The device works; the pair fall in love. When Marshall gets serious enough to insist they marry, Dolores declines as it would interfere with her career. She resumes the affair with her old boyfriend, who has just returned from South America, but finally unable to resist Everett Marshall's love song, she melts, deciding that he is the one after all.

I Live for Love contains five songs by Wrubel and Dixon. Mostly ballads sung by Marshall, none of them became popular. The best is the love song "Mine Alone." The others are the title song, "Silver Wings," "I Wanna Play House," and "A Man Must Shave." The film is a typical light product of its time and did exactly the kind of business Warner's had intended.

STARS OVER BROADWAY

A Warner Brothers Picture/1935
Produced by Sam Bischoff
Directed by William Keighley
Screenplay by Jerry Wald and Julius Epstein
Based on a story by Mildren Cram
Photographed by George Barnes
Songs: *Broadway Cinderella*
    Where Am I?
    At Your Service Madame
    You Let Me Down
    Over Yonder Moon
    September in the Rain
       by Al Dubin and Harry Warren

    Carry Me Back to the Lone Prairie
       by Carson J. Robison

Dances directed by Busby Berkeley

Running time: 90 minutes

Cast:
Al McGillevray	Pat O'Brien
Jan King	James Melton
Joan Garrett	Jane Froman
Norma Wyman	Jean Muir
Offkey Cramer	Frank McHugh
Romeo	Phil Regan
Minotti	William Ricciardi
Molly	Marie Wilson
Announcer	Frank Fay
Crane	E. E. Clive
Freddie	Eddie Conrad

Stars Over Broadway is another in the Warner Brothers catalogue of backstage musicals. It is best remembered as the film in which Dubin and Warren's "September in the Rain" was introduced. The film also introduced the now classic Western ballad, "Carry Me Back to the Lone Prairie," by folk singer Carson J. Robison.

Both James Melton, a popular concert and operatic tenor, and co-star Jane Froman were well known for their radio broadcasts. This was their first appearance on film. Unfortunately, their many listeners apparently did not turn out in large enough numbers to justify Warner's or any other studio again building a feature around them.

Hard-working Pat O'Brien appears as a fast-talking manipulator, a talent manager who turns Melton from a hotel porter into a radio star. O'Brien manages his protégé for a fifty percent commission and discourages his natural bent toward opera, insisting that there is quick and easy money to be made in radio. Melton becomes demoralized, hitting the skids and the bottle, until at last O'Brien relents and sends the young tenor off to Italy for some operatic training.

The singing is by far the best part of *Stars Over Broadway*, with Melton having the lion's share. The film was a minor assignment for Busby Berkeley requiring a few fairly routine dance ensembles, none particularly memorable. There was a comedy setting for "At Your Service Madame," and another production in a nightclub—the kind of nightclub possible only in Hollywood musicals since it required floor space the area of an airplane hangar. Berkeley remembers the film with a tinge of regret because he had planned an elaborate setting for "September in the Rain," complete with a forest of movable silver trees, but the front office decided the cost of the idea was out of line with the probable returns on *Stars Over Broadway*, and the idea was abandoned.

James Melton, Metropolitan Opera tenor, vocalizes for maestro Frank McHugh as Pat O'Brien looks on.

Jane Froman, famous radio singer, in a production sequence.

STAGE STRUCK

A Warner Brothers Picture/1936
Produced by Robert Lord
Directed by Busby Berkeley
Screenplay by Tom Buckingham and Pat C. Flick
Based on a story by Robert Lord
Photographed by Byron Haskin
Songs: *In Your Own Quiet Way*
   Fancy Meeting You
   You're Kinda Grandish
   The New Parade
    by E. Y. Harburg and Harold Arlen

Running time: 90 minutes

Cast:
George Randall	Dick Powell
Peggy Revere	Joan Blondell
Fred Harris	Warren William
Sid	Frank McHugh
Ruth Williams	Jeanne Madden
Grace	Carol Hughes
Gilmore Frost	Craig Reynolds
Wayne	Hobart Cavanaugh
Oscar Freud	Johnnie Arthur
Mrs. Randall	Spring Byington
Dr. Stanley	Thomas Pogue
Burns Heywood	Andrew Tombes
Toots O'Connor	Lulu McConnell
Cooper	Val Stanton
Marley	Ernie Stanton

Stage Struck was given a badly needed boost at the box office when Dick Powell and Joan Blondell got married just before its release. Another backstage musical, this one tried to poke fun at "the show must go on" tradition. Like *42nd Street*, it recounts the old story of the unknown kid who makes good as the last minute fill-in for the star.

Joan Blondell is the stage star with little talent but plenty of nerve. She backs herself in a musical show with Dick Powell as the director. A clash of temperament ends the enterprise but Powell finds himself stuck with her again in his next job. Warren William, ever the smooth gent, is the show's producer. He reconciles the pair by playing up to Blondell's pretensions to culture and intellectual snobbery. Frank McHugh, one of Warner's hardest working actors, is Powell's goofy assistant, echoing his boss's stage instructions. A quartet, the Yacht Club boys, perform in two of the musical numbers—one with acrobatic high-jinks in the producer's office accompanied by some nifty Harburg lyrics. Their other routine is a strictly topical bit about politics and taxes although its digs at the government's rising tax rate would seem to apply to any era.

Stage Struck is short on musical production numbers for a Berkeley picture. Warner's was obviously relying on Dick Powell's popularity. His Decca recordings of the film's two main songs—"Fancy Meeting You" and "In Your Own Quiet Way"—and his use of them on his broadcasts no doubt helped *Stage Struck* to clear a profit. Both are fine songs by the team of Harburg and Arlen, yet neither became standards. Berkeley staged "Fancy Meeting You" in a museum as Powell sang Harburg's lyrical references to evolution to ingenue Jeanne Madden.

> *Remember when the world began?*
> *I was your prehistoric man?*

Stage Struck was the second of three films for which Warner's had signed Harburg and Arlen. The first was Al Jolson's *The Singing Kid*, and the last was also Busby Berkeley's next assignment, *The Gold Diggers of 1937*.

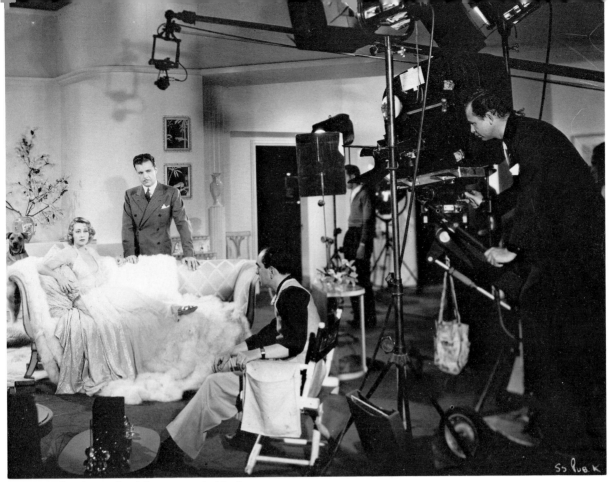

Dick Powell and Joan Blondell, on a sea of white fox, listen to director Berkeley.

Director Berkeley inspects the chorus line.

Joan Blondell, whose personality and verve come through so brilliantly in Berkeley's films, shown here before the curtain with Busby.

GOLD DIGGERS OF 1937

A Warner Brothers—First National Picture
Produced by Hal B. Wallis
Directed by Lloyd Bacon
Screenplay by Warren Duff
Based on a play by Richard Maibaum, Michael
   Wallach, and George Haight
Photographed by Arthur Edeson
Songs: *With Plenty of Money and You*
   All's Fair in Love and War
      by Al Dubin and Harry Warren

   Speaking of the Weather
   Let's Put Our Heads Together
   Life Insurance Song
   Hush Ma Mouth
      by E. Y. Harburg and Harold Arlen

Numbers created and directed by Busby Berkeley
Running time: 100 minutes
Cast: Rosmer Peek .... Dick Powell
   Norma Perry .... Joan Blondell
   J. J. Hobart .... Victor Moore
   Genevieve Larkin .... Glenda Farrell
   Boop Oglethorpe .... Lee Dixon
   Morty Wethered .... Osgood Perkins
   Sally .... Rosalind Marquis
   Hugo .... Charles D. Brown
   Irene .... Irene Ware
   Andy Callahan .... William Davidson
   Dr. MacDuffy .... Olin Howland
   Dr. Bell .... Charles Halton
   Dr. Warshof .... Paul Irving
   Dr. Henry .... Harry C. Bradley
   Chairman .... Joseph Crehan

The *Gold Diggers of 1937* kept up the tradition of Warner's expensive musicals. Sets and scenes were again lavish and there was a little more stress on comedy. The screenplay reworked a stage play, *Sweet Mystery of Life*, about backstage machinations in the theatre, that had been presented in New York the previous year. Warner's spiked it with more jibes at show business and leavened it with music.

Dick Powell, by now one of Hollywood's brightest singing stars, plays a confident insurance salesman bamboozled by a pair of chiselers, Osgood Perkins and Charles D. Brown. They talk him into selling a million-dollar policy to a hypochondriac theatrical producer, played with scene-stealing ease by Victor Moore. Moore seems about to expire momentarily, and when Powell realizes the fraud, he puts all his energy into keeping the producer in good health and spirits. Showgirl-turned-secretary, Joan Blondell, whose former interest in show business is revitalized by Powell, and some of her girl friends assist him and succeed so well that Moore turns into a gay old codger, leaving Powell, a show-biz type at heart, to take over production of the show, with Blondell as his star.

Joan Blondell had been popular more as a comedienne than as a glamour girl. Now linked in private life with Dick Powell, she became more chic. Her skill with light comedy continued to make her more interesting than most of Powell's other co-stars.

The score of the picture is the work of two pairs of songwriters. Al Dubin and Harry Warren provide the theme song, "With Plenty of Money and You," which opens the picture, and "All's Fair in Love and War" which closes it. Sandwiched between are four songs by E. Y. Harburg and Harold Arlen. Powell recorded all four of the songs, although the Dubin and Warren songs were more popular and more direct in their appeal than the subtle musicianship of lyrics and melodies by Harburg and Arlen.

Busby Berkeley didn't have to work as hard on *The Gold Diggers of 1937* as on previous blockbuster Warner musicals. Most of his efforts were concentrated on two production numbers. The charming "Let's Put Our Heads Together" is staged in a garden as a summer party. The goings-on are much more decorous than those in "Pettin' in the Park" from *The Gold Diggers of 1933*. The girls in the garden are supplemented by fifty big white rocking chairs, each chair holding a happy pair of lovers.

The film's finale gives Berkeley another opportunity to display his propensity for military drill. With Joan Blondell in the lead, seventy girls in fetching white uniforms, carrying flags and drums, march through innumerable formations on the shiny black floor. Skillful lighting and ace camera work make the sequence startlingly realistic. The catchy marching song, "All's Fair in Love and War," contains Al Dubin's comment on the methods of the distaff side:

> And with your back against the wall,
> She marches you to City Hall and leads you
>   through the door,
> And then the deed is done, her victory is
>   won,
> For love is just like war.

Whatever their motives, the marching Berkeley girls win a definite cinematic and choreographic victory with the finale of *The Gold Diggers of 1937*.

Powell orders an advance in a musical war between the sexes.

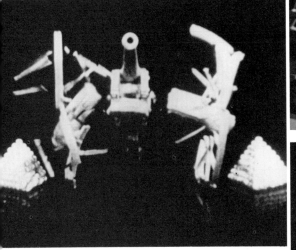

A cannon explodes; the pieces converge to become two couples in a rocking chair—a spectacular surrealistic effect.

Another cannon fires--the cannonball explodes into an image of Joan Blondell.

Super-colossal props made Berkeley's films truly larger than life, a play of scale and reality in pursuit of fantasy.

THE GO-GETTER

A Cosmopolitan—Warner Brothers Production/1937
Produced by Hal B. Wallis
Associate Producer, Sam Bischoff
Directed by Busby Berkeley
Screenplay by Delmer Daves
Based on a story by Peter B. Kyne
Photographed by Arthur Edeson
Song: *It Shall Be Done*
       by Jack Scholl and M. K. Jerome

Running time: 90 minutes
Cast: Bill Austin . . . . George Brent
       Margaret Ricks . . . . Anita Louise
       Cappy Ricks . . . . Charles Winninger
       Lloyd Skinner . . . . John Eldridge
       Commander Tisdale . . . . Henry O'Neill
       Karl Stone . . . . Joseph Crehan
       Matt Peasley . . . . Willard Robertson
       Lester . . . . Herbert Rawlinson
       Policeman . . . . Ed Gargan

The Go-Getter is typical of the films in which Warner's featured their stars of second magnitude. It is a fast-moving, romantic comedy starring George Brent and Anita Louise, who are backed up by some of the durable actors Warner's kept working almost incessantly under long-term contract.

The Go-Getter opens with a dramatic sequence showing the crash of a U.S. Navy dirigible, in which sailor George Brent loses a leg. Determined not to let this misfortune curb his ambition or dampen his confidence, he gets a job as a salesman for Ricks Lumber and Navigation Company, proving himself a true go-getter and passing every test set for him by his irascible employer. He woos and wins Ricks's lovely daughter, Anita Louise, who accompanies him overseas as manager of the Shanghai division of the Ricks Company. With Winninger's operation crippled by a strike, Brent returns to heroically settle the problem and take control of management, finally convincing his father-in-law that both his daughter and his business are in capable hands.

The story was originally filmed as a silent in 1923 by Cosmopolitan, one of the independent companies Warner's brought into its fold. Screenwriter Delmer Daves made some changes in the Peter B. Kyne story for this version, playing up the comedy and allowing Charles Winninger to shine in the role of Cappy Ricks, a character who appears in several Kyne stories and films made from them. The part of the lovable curmudgeon with a rough manner and a heart of gold suited Winninger perfectly.

Charles Winninger and George Brent in a scene from the film.

"Night Over Shanghai" from *The Singing Marine*.
Chinese Chippendale à la Berkeley, undulating complete
with human arms—an effect worthy of Jean Cocteau.

THE SINGING MARINE

A Warner Brothers Picture/1937
Directed by Ray Enright
With two sequences directed by Busby Berkeley
Screenplay by Delmer Daves
Photographed by Arthur L. Todd
Songs: *'Cause My Baby Says It's So*
　　　I Know Now
　　　Night Over Shanghai (lyrics by Johnny Mercer)
　　　The Lady Who Couldn't Be Kissed
　　　You Can't Run Away From Love Tonight
　　　The Song of the Marines
　　　　by Al Dubin and Harry Warren

Running time: 105 minutes

Cast:　Bob Brent . . . . Dick Powell
　　　Peggy Randall . . . . Doris Weston
　　　Slim Baxter . . . . Lee Dixon
　　　Aeneas Phinney . . . . Hugh Herbert
　　　Ma Marine . . . . Jane Darwell
　　　Sergeant Mike . . . . Allen Jenkins
　　　"Doc" Rockwell . . . George "Doc" Rockwell
　　　Larry Adler . . . . Himself
　　　Fanny Hatteras . . . . Rose King
　　　Helen Young . . . . Marcia Ralston
　　　Dopey . . . . Guinn (Big Boy) Williams
　　　Diane . . . . Veda Ann Borg
　　　Joan . . . . Jane Wyman
　　　J. Montgomery Madison . . . Berton Churchill

Two of Dick Powell's most successful musicals
had military themes. In *Flirtation Walk* he had been
a West Point cadet, and in *Don't Give Up The Ship*,
an Annapolis midshipman. Ruby Keeler had co-
starred in both. It was only a question of time before
Powell turned up in Marine uniform. The script required Powell to take the film's title literally, deliver-
ing five of the six songs. Two of them were greatly
aided by the fanciful hand of Busby Berkeley.

Powell plays a bashful young Marine from Arkan-
sas whose barrack-room buddies send him off to
enter a radio program talent contest. Taking a fur-
lough from the Marine base in San Diego, Powell
proceeds to New York with his girl friend, who is
also a singer. She flops, but he clicks and quickly
skyrockets to fame as "The Singing Marine." When
success goes to his head, he loses his girl and his
buddies. Eventually he falls back into line, recover-
ing his humility and deciding he would rather be a
Marine than an entertainer.

"Night Over Shanghai" is staged in a nightclub
with the set expanded to allow street scenes and a
basement cabaret. Bits of dramatic action spike the
music. Larry Adler, the champion harmonica player
of his day, opens the number with a pin spotlight on
his hands as he plays. The effect is rather like a flut-
tering butterfly. The spotlight broadens to reveal the
Shanghai nightery with Powell singing a song reminiscent of "Limehouse Blues."

The Singing Marine is one more musical that
hangs on its songs: six from Harry Warren, five with
lyrics by Al Dubin, and one by Johnny Mercer. Powell recorded four of them for Decca. He did particularly well with "Cause My Baby Says It's So," and
"The Song of the Marines," which was officially
adopted by the Marine Corps.

Varsity Show is so collegiate that even the band's chairs are red striped! Here Fred Waring and His Pennsylvanians perform "Love Is On the Air Tonight."

VARSITY SHOW

A Warner Brothers Picture/1937
Directed by William Keighley
Screenplay by Jerry Wald, Richard Macauley, Sig
 Herzig, and Warren Duff
Photographed by Sol Polito
Songs: *Have You Got Any Castles, Baby?*
 Love Is On the Air Tonight
 Moonlight on the Campus
 Old King Cole
 On With the Dance
 We're Working Our Way Through College
 You've Got Something There
 When Your College Days Are Gone
  by Johnny Mercer and Richard Whiting

Finale created and directed by Busby Berkeley
Running time: 120 minutes
Cast: Charles "Chuck" Daly . . . . Dick Powell
  Ernie Mason . . . . Fred Waring
  Betty Bradley . . . . Priscilla Lane
  Prof. Sylvester Biddle . . . . Walter Catlett
  William Williams . . . . Ted Healy
  Barbara Steward . . . . Rosemary Lane
  Buzz Bolton . . . . Johnny Davis
  Johnny "Rubberlegs" Stevens . . . . Lee Dixon
  Cuddles . . . . Mabel Todd
  Hap . . . . George MacFarland
  Dean Meredith . . . . Halliwell Hobbs
  Mike Barclay . . . . Ed Brophy
  Mrs. Smith . . . . Emma Dunn
  Buck and Bubbles . . . . Themselves
  Trout . . . . Sterling Holloway

Varsity Show is the most musical of the Warner musicals, and the longest—two hours. Lyricist Johnny Mercer and composer Richard Whiting contributed eight new songs and the picture also uses a medley of college tunes.

The undergraduates of Winfield College are about to stage their annual show but badly need a producer to whip their ragged efforts into shape. Someone remembers Dick Powell, the successful Broadway producer, as an outstanding Winfield alumnus. After much persuasion he agrees to return to the ivy-covered halls to salvage the show. The head of Winfield's music department, Fred Waring, well known with the Pennsylvanians for his college routines and his radio program, supplies musical entertainment.

The finale is a landslide of musical effort. "The set covered a whole sound stage. It centered on a giant staircase fifty feet high and sixty feet wide, on which I paraded my entire company of several hundred boys and girls. The object of the number was to salute the leading colleges and universities, including the military and naval academies, and in my overhead shots I had them form the initials and insignias of the various institutions. Each formation had a musical accompaniment, mostly variations on the campus originals. It was an exhausting number to stage and rehearse, but well worth the effort because it brought down the house almost everywhere it was shown."

HOLLYWOOD HOTEL

A Warner Brothers—First National Picture/1937
Produced by Hal B. Wallis
Directed by Busby Berkeley
Screenplay by Jerry Wald, Maurice Leo, and
  Richard Macauley
Photographed by Charles Rosher and George Barnes
Songs: *Can't Teach My Heart New Tricks*
      I'm Like a Fish Out of Water
      I've Hitched My Wagon to a Star
      Let That Be a Lesson to You
      Silhouetted in the Moonlight
      Sing You Son of a Gun
      Hooray for Hollywood
        by Johnny Mercer and Richard A. Whiting

Running time: 103 minutes

Cast:
Ronnie Bowers	Dick Powell
Virginia	Rosemary Lane
Mona Marshall	Lola Lane
Fuzzy	Ted Healy
Georgia	Johnny Davis
Alexander Dupre	Alan Mowbray
Alice	Frances Langford
Louella Parsons	Herself
Chester Marshall	Hugh Herbert
Jonesy	Glenda Farrell
Ken Nyles	Himself
Bernie Walton	Allyn Joslyn
Callaghan	Edgar Kennedy
Dress Designer	Curt Bois
Cameraman	Eddie Acuff
Dot Marshall	Mabel Todd
Jerry Cooper	Himself

Hollywood Hotel is all Berkeley. Packed with songs, comedy, and romance, it was released in time for the Christmas season of 1937. *Hollywood Hotel*, lively and amusing, met with a ready audience. The picture was based on the extremely successful radio program of the same name, which starred Dick Powell, Frances Langford, and movie-gossip columnist Louella Parsons.

Hollywood studios and the broadcasting industry of 1937 get a good-natured ribbing in the film; even the lyrics of its theme song, "Hooray for Hollywood," are tongue-in-cheek:

> *Hooray for Hollywood, that screwy,*
>   *bally-hooey Hollywood.*
> *Where any office boy or young mechanic*
>   *can be a panic,*
> *With just a good-looking pan.*
> *And any barmaid can be a star made,*
> *If she dances with or without a fan.*

Perhaps the most devastating line in the song is: "Hooray for Hollywood, where you're terrific if you're even good."

Dick Powell breezes through the picture with ease. "Dick was one of the finest men I ever knew in Hollywood and he never changed in all the time I knew him. He was entirely businesslike in what he did. I never saw or heard of his being unpleasant or difficult. His death at fifty-eight was a tremendous loss to the industry, both as a creator and as a backbone."

The films Busby Berkeley made for Warner's after *Hollywood Hotel* were much less grandiose in scope and cost, as were Dick Powell's *Hard to Get* and *Naughty But Nice*. *Hollywood Hotel* seemed to suggest to Warner's that they had gone as far as they could with their cycle of lavish musicals.

Dick Powell and Lola Lane, wading in a fountain, sing "I'm Like a Fish Out of Water." (Notice Powell's garters peeking from beneath his trousers!)

MEN ARE SUCH FOOLS

A Warner Brothers Picture/1938
Directed by Busby Berkeley
Associate Producer, David Lewis
Screenplay by Norman Reilly Raine and
   Horace Jackson
Based on the novel by Faith Baldwin
Photographed by Sid Hickox
Musical score by Heinz Roemheld
Running time: 70 minutes

Cast: Jimmy Hall . . . . Wayne Morris
   Linda Lawrence . . . . Priscilla Lane
   Harry Galleon . . . . Humphrey Bogart
   Harvey Bates . . . . Hugh Herbert
   Nancy . . . . Penny Singleton
   Tad . . . . Johnny Davis
   Beatrice Harris . . . . Mona Barrie
   Wanda Townsend . . . . Marcia Ralston
   Bill Dalton . . . . Gene Lockhart
   Mrs. Dalton . . . . Kathleen Lockhart
   George Onslow . . . . Donald Briggs
   Mrs. Pinkel . . . . Renie Riano
   Rudolf . . . . Claude Allister
   Mrs. Nelson . . . . Nedda Harrigan
   Mr. Nelson . . . . Eric Stanley
   Bill Collyer . . . . James Nolan
   June Cooper . . . . Carole Landis

Men Are Such Fools was one of six pictures released in 1938 in which Humphrey Bogart appeared, although it was not a major vehicle for him. Top billing went to Wayne Morris, who was being futilely promoted as a popular leading man. His co-star was Priscilla Lane, who also never quite made it as a box-office attraction.

Priscilla Lane plays an ambitious girl who lands a job as an account executive with an advertising agency. She falls in love with ex-football star, Wayne Morris, whom she agrees to marry provided she does not have to give up her career. Bogart, her boss, cares nothing for either marriage vows or business ethics and tries to buy her affection with offers of promotions. When the husband becomes jealous, she resigns from the promising job to devote herself to him and their home, but becoming disenchanted with her husband's seeming lack of ambition, she leaves him and returns to her job—to Bogart's delight. The challenged husband decides to launch himself in the business world and after a year without word from him she decides to get a divorce in order to marry Bogart. When the husband learns of this he begs his wife to reconsider and a reconciliation takes place, leaving Bogart to look for other companionship.

Humphrey Bogart made his first film in 1930, ten years after he began his stage career. Unhappy with his assignments in Hollywood, he drifted back to New York where his success came in 1934 with the role of Duke Mantee, the gangster in *The Petrified Forest*. Two years later Warner's made the film version, and Bogart repeated the role for the screen, sketching such an indelible picture of a tough, menacing villain that the image marked him for the rest of his life.

Men Are Such Fools was just one of a score of pictures in which Bogart appeared before he was recognized as a powerful screen actor with a distinct personality. Recalls Busby Berkeley, "Bogie was never any trouble to me at all. He felt, and I agreed with him, that he should be working in better films, but whatever discontent he felt, he took out on the bosses, not on the people he was working with. As far as I know, he never refused to play a part. His credo was to keep working, and I agreed with him on that point, too."

Men Are Such Fools, and Humphrey Bogart was one of them, shown here in a tender moment with Priscilla Lane.

Professor Berkeley shows the formation sequence for the Latin Quarter number to some of the chorus from *Gold Diggers in Paris*.

La Vie Parisienne in Berkeley's eyes became a line of fetching young American beauties.

GOLD DIGGERS IN PARIS

A Warner Brothers Picture/1938
Produced by Sam Bischoff
Directed by Ray Enright
Screenplay by Earl Baldwin and Warren Duff
Based on a story by Jerry Wald, Richard Macauley,
  and Maurice Leo
Photographed by Sol Polito and George Barnes
Songs: *The Latin Quarter*
       I Wanna Go Back to Bali
       A Stranger in Paree
       Put That Down in Writing
            by Al Dubin and Harry Warren

       Day Dreaming All Night Long
       Waltz of the Flowers
       My Adventure
            by Johnny Mercer and Harry Warren

Numbers staged and directed by Busby Berkeley
Running time: 100 minutes
Cast: Terry Moore . . . . Rudy Vallee
      Kay Morrow . . . . Rosemary Lane
      Maurice Giraud . . . . Hugh Herbert
      Duke Dennis . . . . Allen Jenkins
      Mona . . . . Gloria Dickson
      Pierre LeBrec . . . . Melville Cooper
      Leticia . . . . Mabel Todd
      Luis Leoni . . . . Fritz Feld
      Mike Coogan . . . . Ed Brophy
      Padrinski . . . . Curt Bois
      Gendarme . . . . Victor Killian
      Doorman . . . . Eddie Anderson

Rudy Vallee was another of the tremendously popular radio stars of the 1930's who was never able to win the same degree of acceptance in films. *The Gold Diggers in Paris* was the first film he had made in three years, and although the reviewers thought it was his best, it still did little to make him a box-office draw. Ironically, Vallee would later become a busy character actor, starting with Preston Sturges's *The Palm Beach Story*, stressing comedy and dropping his singing. But in *The Gold Diggers in Paris* Vallee is the romantic, singing leading man, with a fondness for impersonating Maurice Chevalier and FDR.

For Busby Berkeley the film presented a challenge in that he had to stage his musical numbers with less expense. "This had always been a problem at Warner's even though the musicals were making fortunes for them. I had to fight to get good budgets for my productions and the executives were always nagging me to reduce costs. When we were filming *The Gold Diggers of 1937*, Hal Wallis drew the line on any more expensive sets. I was so damned mad I figured out a way of showing them I could stage an extravaganza with no set at all. 'All's Fair in Love and War' was done with nothing but a sound-stage floor covered with shiny black surfacing. And that particular number was nominated for an Academy Award, which gave me great satisfaction." Three other Berkeley production numbers were nominated for Oscars—"The Lullaby of Broadway," and "The Words Are in My Heart" routines in *The Gold Diggers of 1935*, and the finale of *Varsity Show*. But awards for dance direction were dropped by the Academy after 1937.

The Gold Diggers in Paris leans heavily on the old plot devices of misunderstanding and mistaken identity. A French envoy invites Rudy Vallee and his

nightclub dancing ensemble to partake in the Paris Exposition, mistakenly thinking them to be the American Ballet Company. The Vallee troupe not only manages to compete in the international dance festival, but actually overwhelms the American Ballet Company. The situation gave Berkeley room for a vast amount of precision dancing. Good comedy bits are contributed by Curt Bois as an egocentric ballet genius and Ed Brophy as a gangster patron of the ballet.

The music for *The Gold Diggers in Paris* was provided by Harry Warren. Lyrics to four songs were written by Al Dubin and the others by Johnny Mercer. Mercer's star was now on the ascendant, with Dubin growing increasingly tired of the business. After one more picture with Warren, Dubin abandoned songwriting and drifted away from Hollywood. He died in 1945. Berkeley recalls, "He was a strange man, a kind-hearted man behind a gruff exterior. Al was big and rather sloppy; he smoked cigars and the ash dripped down his vest. You would look at him and wonder how such beautiful lyrics would come out of such an unlikely-looking character. And he was terribly sensitive. He once came on the set to see me while I was doing a routine. I was very busy and I must have spoken brusquely to him. Al just walked out of the studio, drove to the railway station, and got on a train for New York. I remember I needed another stanza for 'Shuffle Off to Buffalo,' and he wired it to me. Al was a marvelous lyricist,

but he didn't seem to think much of his work. He once said to me that if songwriting was an art, then it was the lowest form. But Al was witty, knowledgeable, and deft. One of the best songs in this picture was 'I Wanna Go Back to Bali,' with Vallee singing the praises of the island paradise. If you listen closely you'll hear:

> *I've seen those scenes in magazines,*
> *But they never do show the flies.*

Al Dubin probably sensed that the Warner musical bonanza was running out and he wasn't interested enough to pursue it with any other studio. I guess we all realized that an era was coming to an end. The next year, when Harry Warren and Dick Powell and I all left Warner's, it did."

Rudy Vallee in the "I Wanna Go Back to Bali" production. Slashed budgets reduced the spectacle, but Berkeley shows his mettle with admirable style.

The recurrent military motif again in this sequence from the finale.

GARDEN OF THE MOON

A Warner Brothers Picture/1938
Directed by Busby Berkeley
Screenplay by Jerry Wald and Richard Macauley
Based on a story by H. Bedford-Jones and
    Barton Browne
Photographed by Tony Gaudio
Songs: *Garden of the Moon*
        The Girl Friend of the Whirling Dervish
        Love is Where You Find It
        The Lady on the Two-Cent Stamp
        Confidentially
            by Al Dubin and Harry Warren

Running time: 94 minutes
Cast: John Quinn .... Pat O'Brien
      Toni Blake .... Margaret Lindsay
      Don Vincente .... John Payne
      Slappy Harris .... Johnnie Davis
      Maurice .... Melville Cooper
      Mrs. Lornay .... Isabel Jeans
      Mary Stanton .... Mabel Todd
      Miss Calder .... Penny Singleton
      Rick Fulton .... Dick Purcell
      Maharajah of Sund .... Curt Bois
      Angus McGillicuddy .... Granville Bates
      Duncan McGillicuddy .... Edward McWade
      Trent .... Larry Williams
      With Joe Venuti and His Swing Cats

Garden of the Moon is a bright musical, with good dialogue and nimble direction from Busby Berkeley. Although none of the five songs written for the picture by Dubin and Warren achieved lasting popularity, they all serve entertainingly within the framework of the film. The sprightly "Girl Friend of the Whirling Dervish" is the kind of ditty that song buffs like to collect. The film's title relates to a nightclub of that name, in which a great deal of the action takes place.

Once again, Pat O'Brien is at his tough-talking best as the ruthless proprietor of the bistro. Young John Payne is the unknown band leader hired as a fill-in, who remains to become successful. The love interest is supplied by press-agent Margaret Lindsay, who falls for the handsome band leader and invents publicity stories to help his career. The story is greatly aided by the humorous play and the steady parade of songs and dances.

An unusual feature of *Garden of the Moon* is the inclusion of plugs for the foremost newspaper columnists of the day. Hollywood's radio and magazine reporter Jimmy Fidler appeared as himself, although more than one unkind critic remarked that it might have been better had someone else played the part. At one point almost all the column titles and by-lines in American journalism of the time are flashed on the screen.

Garden of the Moon launched John Payne's film career, but before Warner's could exercise their option, Twentieth Century–Fox stepped in and signed him to a long-term contract.

The film was Busby Berkeley's last musical for Warner's under his contract. His next two pictures for them would be without music. Warner's policy regarding musicals changed by this time, and the studio had decided to drastically curtail their production in this area.

Pat O'Brien and Margaret Lindsay in a publicity still from the film.

Kay Francis and Ian Hunter in a scene from *Comet Over Broadway*. With luck, this comet won't appear again over Broadway for another seventy-six years.

COMET OVER BROADWAY

A First National–Warner Brothers Production/1938
Associate producer, Bryan Foy
Directed by Busby Berkeley
Screenplay by Mark Hellinger and Robert Buckner
Based on a story by Faith Baldwin
Photographed by James Wong Howe
Musical score by Heinz Roemheld

Cast: Eve Appleton . . . . Kay Francis
Bert Ballin . . . . Ian Hunter
Bill Appleton . . . . John Litel
Joe Grant . . . . Donald Crisp
Tim Adams . . . . Minna Gombell
Jacqueline Appleton . . . . Sybil Jason
Emerson . . . . Melville Cooper
Wilton Banks . . . . Ian Keith
Janet Eaton . . . . Leona Maricle
Tim Brogan . . . . Ray Mayer
Mrs. Appleton . . . . Vera Lewis
Burlesque Manager . . . . Nat Carr
Willis . . . . Chester Clute
Harvey . . . . Edward McWade
Lem . . . . Clem Bevans
Miss McDermott . . . . Linda Winters

Very much a woman's picture, *Comet Over Broadway* was based on a *Cosmopolitan* magazine short story by Faith Baldwin. The protagonist was played by Kay Francis, an actress of dark and dignified beauty, who had built her career largely on portraying women who suffer quietly and nobly.

Looking back on his association with her in *Comet Over Broadway*, Busby Berkeley recalls, "Kay had a reputation for being a bit difficult. I had been told by other directors that she had sometimes been tactless with co-workers and studio executives, but I saw no evidence of it on this picture. I do know she was unwilling to participate in the publicity game. That didn't interest her at all. And it seemed to me she lacked that driving ambition an actress needs in order to get the best parts in the best films. I found her to be cooperative and humorous, perhaps because she knew this was one of her last films for Warner's. She had been under contract since 1932 at the rate of four pictures a year, and I think she was rather glad the grind was coming to an end."

Comet Over Broadway is, by intent, sentimental and melodramatic. Kay Francis appears as a young married woman obsessed by her ambition to be an actress. Her association with a Broadway actor (Keith) leads to his murder by her jealous husband (Litel), for which the husband gets a life sentence. Dedicating herself to making his fate easier, she strives to have him paroled and eventually secures his freedom. Motivated by the need for money, she takes any kind of work—in carnivals, burlesque, vaudeville. Deprived of a Broadway opportunity by a rival actress, she goes to London and becomes a success on the stage there. Thanks to the interest of a gentlemanly theatrical producer (Hunter), she gets a chance to shine on Broadway. But at the moment of triumph, word arrives that her husband is being let out of jail on parole. Kay becomes emotionally pulled in three directions—her career, her deepening affection for the producer, and her loyalty to a husband who badly needs her. In true soap-opera style, the promising career and true love are sacrificed by the dutiful wife.

In *Comet Over Broadway* Busby Berkeley showed what he could do with a non-musical, non-comedic story; his next directing job would be an even more dramatic and hard-hitting property.

BROADWAY SERENADE

An MGM Picture/1939
Produced and directed by Robert Z. Leonard
Screenplay by Charles Lederer
Based on a story by Lew Lipton, Hans Kraly, and John
   Tainter Foote
Photographed by Oliver T. Marsh
Musical direction by Herbert Stothart
Finale created and directed by Busby Berkeley
Running time: 118 minutes
Cast: Mary Hale . . . . Jeanette MacDonald
      Jimmy Allen . . . . Lew Ayres
      Cornelius Collier . . . . Frank Morgan
      Larry Bryant . . . . Ian Hunter
      Judy . . . . Rita Johnson
      Pearl . . . . Virginia Grey
      Bob . . . . William Gargan
      Ingalls . . . . Katherine Alexander

Broadway Serenade is one of the less well-remembered films of Jeanette MacDonald, possibly because she had no famous co-star and hence no duets. In the list of her films it falls chronologically between *Sweethearts* and *New Moon*, both very successful features with Nelson Eddy. Here she is paired with Lew Ayres, somewhat lost as a temperamental musician. By then Ayres had made *Young Dr. Kildare*, and it was in the long string of sequels to that film that he found his niche and popularity.

Broadway Serenade lacks the consistency of a musical score from a single source. The songs are a mixed bag, including some from the 1890's, the era in which the story is set, and new ones by Sigmund Romberg, Walter Donaldson, and Herbert Stothart, all with lyrics by Gus Kahn. It was decided that the film badly needed a smash finale and the obvious choice to create it was Busby Berkeley, then free of his Warner Brothers contract.

Jeanette MacDonald and Lew Ayres are married and working in a café as a song-and-piano team. When Ayres knocks down a drunken but influential customer they lose the job. As MacDonald starts to find success as an operatic singer, Ayres can find

The finale—Tchaikovsky's "None But the Lonely Heart"
with Jeanette MacDonald descending the staircase
amid masked players representing famous composers.

work only as a barroom pianist. Sensing a romance between his wife and her producer, he also grows jealous and sullen. The misunderstanding grows into a rift and the couple divorce. Ayres is also a composer and now devotes his time to writing music, eventually coming up with a symphonic fantasy that is, ironically, purchased as a vehicle for his ex-wife. When the work is performed, it meets with great acclaim and also serves to re-unite the couple, who have never stopped loving each other.

Inventing a spectacular finale was particularly difficult for Berkeley because he was brought in after most of the film had been completed, and the producer had almost no idea of what he wanted. The segment was to be ten minutes of screen time and would be accompanied by a symphonic work Herbert Stothart had made from Tchaikovsky's song "None But the Lonely Heart." "They wanted the thing created in short order because Jeanette had to leave. I put on my thinking cap and came up with an idea that would tell how the composer was inspired to write the piece after hearing a melody played by a shepherd. I had the art director build

me a huge set in varying elevations, all covered with black oilcloth. I wanted a hundred musicians and thirty male singers dressed in black frocks and wearing specially made Benda masks to represent all the great composers. Then there would be twenty female singers dressed in simple flowing black dresses, with Jeanette wearing a beautiful cape and gown. After the composer has heard the shepherd's melody, he sets to work transforming it into a symphony. This gave me a transition—with the completed composition I had my musicians in full dress banked high on the left of the screen with the boy and girl singers in evening suits and gowns on the right of the screen—all of this surrounding a thirty-foot-high pedestal on which Jeanette stood and sang her lyrics. I again insisted on using only one camera but I had it mounted on a large boom with the cameraman and myself on either side and I made that thing practically float through the air."

Berkeley had been signed by MGM only for this one production, but on the strength of this film they offered him a substantial contract with yearly options.

Jeanette MacDonald, without Nelson Eddy, atop a column as the camera boom swings out to catch the action.

BABES IN ARMS

An MGM Picture/1939
Produced by Arthur Freed
Directed by Busby Berkeley
Screenplay by Jack McGowan and Kay Van Riper
Based on the Rodgers and Hart musical play
Photographed by Ray June
Songs by Richard Rodgers and Lorenz Hart,
    Harold Arlen and E. Y. Harburg,
    Nacio Herb Brown and Arthur Freed
Musical direction by George Stoll
Running time: 94 minutes

Cast:
Mickey Moran	Mickey Rooney
Patsy Barton	Judy Garland
Joe Moran	Charles Winninger
Judge Black	Guy Kibbee
Rosalie Essex	June Preisser
Florrie Moran	Grace Hayes
Molly Moran	Betty Jaynes
Don Brice	Douglas McPhail
Jeff Steele	Rand Brooks
Dody Martini	Leni Lynn
Bobs	John Sheffield
Madox	Henry Hull
William	Barnett Parker
Mrs. Barton	Ann Shoemaker
Martha Steele	Margaret Hamilton
Mr. Essex	Joseph Crehan

Babes in Arms was a hugely successful and auspicious picture. It was lyricist Arthur Freed's first effort as a producer, and marked the beginning of his new career as Hollywood's foremost producer of musicals, all of them with MGM. As Busby Berkeley's first directorial job for MGM it marked a new plateau in his career. The teaming of Mickey Rooney and Judy Garland was the beginning of a new success. Rooney was then among the top ten at the box office and Judy was fresh from her triumph in *The Wizard of Oz.*

The film was based on the Broadway musical *Babes in Arms*, with book, lyrics, and music by Richard Rodgers and Lorenz Hart, which had enjoyed a nine months' run at the Shubert Theatre in 1937. In producing it for the screen Arthur Freed retained only three of the original songs—the title song, "The Lady is a Tramp," and "Where or When"—and added some of his own material, which would become standard practice in Freed musicals. He and Nacio Herb Brown wrote one new number, "Good Morning," and added two old hits—"You Are My Lucky Star" and "I Cried for You." Freed also commissioned E. Y. Harburg and Harold Arlen to write a production song, "God's Country." Harburg and Arlen had recently scored a great success with their melodies for *The Wizard of Oz*, where Freed had acted as an associate to producer Mervyn LeRoy.

The original story line of *Babes in Arms* was altered in order to build up Rooney's part, but the premise remains the same: a group of old vaudevillians try to stage a comeback, which ends up a complete failure. Desperately short of money and faced with dire hardships, the troupers' children come to the rescue by staging their own show. By dint of sheer youthful enthusiasm they overcome all obstacles and manage to get their show on the boards. It is, of course, a knockout.

Babes in Arms met with happy response from the public and critics. The film is fresh, amiable, spirited and is perhaps best summed up by Berkeley's staging of the title song. Mickey, Judy, and all the other show-biz kids march through the streets lustily singing about who they are and what they are going to do: "They call us babes in arms, but we are babes in armor." Just to watch them is to know there is no stopping them.

For Busby Berkeley, the picture was pure vindication. The days of the old Warner spectacles were gone, but another kind of musical had arrived, and MGM would be its chief purveyor.

Garland and Rooney in blackface.

"God's Country." An elaborate production showcasing
the engaging talents of Mickey Rooney and Judy Garland.

Conductor Rooney rehearses the orchestra and chorus.

Ann Sothern, Franchot Tone, and Ruth Hussey, with Allyn Joslyn and Lee Bowman looking on in the background.

FAST AND FURIOUS

An MGM Production/1939
Produced by Frederick Stephani
Directed by Busby Berkeley
Screenplay by Harry Kurnitz
Photographed by Ray June
Musical score by Daniele Amfitheatrof
Running time: 70 minutes
Cast: Joel Sloane .... Franchot Tone
Garda Sloane .... Ann Sothern
Lily Cole .... Ruth Hussey
Mike Stevens .... Lee Bowman
Ted Bentley .... Allyn Joslyn
Eric Bartell .... John Miljan
Ed Connors .... Bernard Nedell
Jerry Lawrence .... Mary Beth Hughes
Sam Travers .... Cliff Clark
Clancy .... James Burke
Capt. Burke .... Frank Orth
Emmy Lou............... Margaret Roach
Miss Brooklyn .... Gladys Blake
Chief Miller .... Granville Bates

Busby Berkeley made it clear to MGM that he wanted to direct not only musicals, but films of all kinds. As his first non-musical assignment, they gave him an excellent feature, *Fast and Furious*, which he directed at a clip that matched the title.

The film's greatest asset is the work of its two leading players—the deft and dapper Franchot Tone, then at the height of his fame, and Ann Sothern, one of the few Hollywood actresses capable of combining sex appeal with humor. In *Fast and Furious* they appear as a well-heeled married couple who are dealers in old books but whose passionate avocation is amateur detective work. This kind of screen fare was popular in the 1930's and 1940's, as best exemplified by the *Thin Man* series.

The screenplay for *Fast and Furious* was supplied by one of the best Hollywood writers, Harry Kurnitz, a man well known for his wit and culture. This story is the kind that holds the audience in suspense until the end, after which the solution to the murder mystery is so obvious that one is piqued at not having guessed the outcome sooner.

The scene of the murder is a seaside city where a bathing beauty contest is underway. Franchot Tone, whose wife is acting playfully jealous, is a judge. In one of the more melodramatic incidents—lending a touch of suspense and fear to the blend of comedy and mystery, the pair is trapped in an elevator shaft as the murderer tries to liquidate them. The first murder, which Tone is trying to solve to get an innocent friend out of jail, is followed by another. Suspects and clues pile up and the gentlemanly Tone gets himself into various predicaments before solving the mystery.

For Ann Sothern, *Fast and Furious* was a happy reunion with Busby Berkeley. She had started as a bit player in his musicals at Warner's in the early 1930's and can easily be spotted in the "Shanghai Lil" sequence of *Footlight Parade*. Berkeley felt that "this picture was a joy to direct."

FORTY LITTLE MOTHERS

An MGM Picture/1940
Produced by Harry Rapf
Directed by Busby Berkeley
Screenplay by Dorothy Yost and Ernest Pagano
Based on a story by Jean Guitton
Photographed by Charles Lawton
Songs: *Little Curly Hair in a High Chair*
        Your Day Will Come
            by Harry Tobias and Nat Simon

Musical Direction by George Stoll
Running time: 87 minutes
Cast: Gilbert Jordan Reed .... Eddie Cantor
      Marian Edwards .... Rita Johnson
      Doris .... Bonita Granville
      Joe Williams .... Ralph Morgan
      Eleanor .... Martha O'Driscoll
      Marcia .... Diana Lewis
      Betty .... Margaret Early
      Lois .... Louise Seidel
      Janette .... Charlotte Munier

Eddie Cantor was never able to duplicate in films his success as a Ziegfeld star on Broadway or his vast following as a radio entertainer. After half a dozen pictures for Samuel Goldwyn, Cantor's film appearances became intermittent. He doubtless grew tired of his typecast image as an eyeball-rolling, hand-clapping buffoon and asked film producers to let him try other kinds of roles. *Forty Little Mothers* is one of the few opportunities he was given. It also brought him back under the guiding hand of Busby Berkeley, who had directed the musical sequences in four of Cantor's films for Goldwyn.

This time neither the star nor the director had to worry about elaborate song-and-dance routines.

In *Forty Little Mothers* Cantor is a lonely college professor down on his luck and out of work. Wandering the waterfront, he dissuades a girl from suicide and manages to get her a job as a waitress. Feeling uplifted by what he has done, he enters a church to pray, only to find an abandoned baby. Cantor is unable to locate the mother; then tries unsuccessfully to deposit the child in an orphanage. Being penniless, he has to steal food and milk in order to feed the child. He is caught, and is brought before a judge who happens to be an old classmate; the sympathetic justice arranges a job for Cantor as a professor at a girls' school. The girls in his class, forty of them, find him a strict taskmaster. When they discover he is harboring a baby in his quarters, they see an opportunity to have him ousted. Cantor berates the girls for their selfishness, and telling them he intends to leave the school of his own accord, the girls beg him to stay. In their change of heart they also want to care for the baby and help hide her from the superintendent, who making the discovery gives Cantor his notice. When the girls mutiny, the superintendent has to reconsider. The baby's mother is then discovered to be the girl Cantor had saved from suicide, is given a job as a secretary at the college, and the story has a happy ending.

Despite a somewhat trite story that borders on the maudlin, *Forty Little Mothers* is a pleasant film, well directed by Berkeley and especially well played by Cantor.

Eddie Cantor, with some of the "little mothers." From left to right: Diana Lewis, Martha O'Driscoll, Bonita Granville, Margaret Early, and Louise Seidel.

STRIKE UP
THE BAND

An MGM Picture/1940
Produced by Arthur Freed
Directed by Busby Berkeley
Screenplay by John Monks, Jr., and Fred Finkelhoffe
Photographed by Ray June
Songs: *Strike Up the Band*
      by George and Ira Gershwin

    Our Love Affair
      by Arthur Freed and Roger Edens

    Drummer Boy
    Nobody
    Do the Conga
    Nell of New Rochelle
      by Roger Edens

Musical direction by George Stoll
Running time: 119 minutes

Cast: Jimmy Connors . . . . Mickey Rooney
       Mary Holden. . . . . Judy Garland
       Paul Whiteman . . . . Himself
       Barbara Frances Morgan . . . . . . June Preisser
       Philip Turner . . . . William Tracy
       Willie Brewster . . . . Larry Nunn
       Annie . . . . Margaret Early
       Mrs. Connors . . . . Ann Shoemaker
       Mr. Judd . . . . Frances Pierlot
       Mrs. May Holden . . . . Virginia Brissac
       Mr. Morgan . . . . George Lessey
       Mrs. Morgan . . . . Enid Bennett
       Doctor . . . . Howard Hickman
       Miss Hodges . . . . Sarah Edwards

With *Babes in Arms* a major success, MGM quickly laid plans for a sequel using much the same talent. *Strike Up the Band* was the result. Jampacked with youthful energy, the film once again proves Mickey Rooney to be a performer beyond comparison—singing, dancing, playing musical instruments, mugging—dominating every minute he is on the screen. Judy Garland is the perfect partner for him—demure and appealing in her acting, beautifully effective in her singing. The film contains a new song written for her by Arthur Freed and Roger Edens, "Our Love Affair," which was to become one of her standards.

Unrelated to the Gershwin musical of the same name except for the use of the title song, the film is about a group of high-school musicians who turn the school band into a swing orchestra aspiring to compete in a national contest conducted by Paul Whiteman.

The gang, trying to raise enough money to get to the audition in Chicago, has their first job playing at the high-school dance, which includes putting on a floor show. By the greatest of coincidences Paul Whiteman and His Orchestra turn up in their own home town to play at the birthday party of rich girl June Preisser, Judy's flirtatious rival for Mickey's affections. Mickey and his band boys attend the party and during a break in the dance, move onto the Whiteman bandstand. When they pick up the instruments, the temptation to play them becomes overpowering, and breaking into music, Rooney does some stunning drumming. Naturally, Whiteman is impressed, and stakes the group with the rest of the money needed to get to the audition. Various silly bits of plot are deployed to hamper the youngsters and fill out the story, but Mickey and Judy finally arrive in Chicago just in time to snatch first prize.

The rapport between Berkeley and Rooney, professionally and personally, is obvious in *Strike Up the Band*. Among the numbers are a conga at the high school dance, and a Victorian melodrama satirically performed by Rooney and Garland, in which some old ballads like "Heaven Will Protect the Working Girl," "The Curse of an Aching Heart," and "I Ain't Got Nobody" are parodied. The picture includes an ingenious little production number. Bragging to Judy how he will arrange and lead the band in the contest, Mickey sets the contents of a fruit dish out on the table and begins his imaginary directing. The fruits dissolve into small puppet musicians playing instruments. The sequence is particularly effective and entertaining.

Strike Up the Band is a showcase for the effervescent Rooney and the dynamic Garland. The finale is built around the title song, a natural and logical piece for this picture, with the cast singing and marching through an elaborate Berkeley military routine. The song reeks of spirit, and in the Berkeley setting it clamors, "Let the drums roll out, let the people shout!"

Garland and Rooney on stage, strutting in a vaudeville routine.

Mickey, Judy, and Busby ponder the musical fruit sequence.

The "Drummer Boy" number with Rooney at the drums.

BLONDE INSPIRATION

An MGM Production
Produced by B. P. Fineman
Directed by Busby Berkeley
Screenplay by Marion Parsonnet
Based on a play by John Cecil Holm
Photographed by Sidney Wagner and
  Oliver T. Marsh
Musical score by Bronislau Kaper
Running time: 71 minutes
Cast: Jonathan Briggs . . . . John Shelton
  Margie Blake . . . . Virginia Grey
  Phil Hendricks . . . . Albert Dekker
  Bittsy Conway . . . . Charles Butterworth
  Dusty King . . . . Donald Meek
  Uncle Reginald . . . . Reginald Owen
  Victoria . . . . Alma Kruger
  Regina . . . . Rita Quigley
  Wanda . . . . Marion Martin
  Mr. Hutchins . . . . George Lessey

Busby Berkeley had gained the reputation as a director with a flair for fast-paced comedy. The musicals made for MGM differed from the early ones at Warner's in more than the absence of elaborate production numbers. Those for MGM were more closely knit, humorous pictures, with the music and the dances better integrated into the story line. MGM, more intent on Berkeley's doing musicals than Warner's had been, occasionally felt obliged to give him a vehicle without music. *Blonde Inspiration* is a case in point.

Blonde Inspiration stars John Shelton, who was unsuccessfully groomed by MGM, and Virginia Grey, who started her movie career as a Berkeley girl at Warner's. Although both perform attractively in this slap-happy story, the real virtuosity comes from such solid character types as Albert Dekker, Charles Butterworth, and Donald Meek. John Shelton, a young timid writer who has spent three years on what he feels is a great novel about the West, can't find any publishers interested enough to take it. In desperation, he leaves the home of his overbearing aunt (Kruger) and his henpecked uncle (Owen) determined to make his way in the literary world. His uncle gives him two thousand dollars to give him a start, and he gets a job as a hack writer for a pulp magazine. The conniving editor (Dekker) learns about the money and sells the budding author a share of *Dusty Trails* magazine. The magazine's top writer (Meek) is a dipsomaniac who can never be relied upon to turn in his copy on time, but since his name sells the magazine, the editor unscrupulously attributes Shelton's stories to him. Helplessly bound by a contract he unwittingly signed, he is consoled and encouraged by the editor's warmhearted, pretty secretary (Grey) who also gives encouragement for a new novel. When the editor steals the novel and issues it under another name, Shelton goes berserk, tries to destroy the magazine's printing shop, and lands in jail. Mistakenly, he thinks his girl friend has also betrayed him, but she is responsible for his manuscript finally appearing under his own name, which in turn leads to a contract with a reputable publishing house. *Blonde Inspiration*, with its humorous and occasionally naughty touches, is narrowly saved from mediocrity by Busby Berkeley's swift direction.

Virginia Grey, John Shelton, Charles Butterworth, and Albert Dekker.

ZIEGFELD
GIRL

ZIEGFELD GIRL

An MGM Picture/1941
Produced by Pandro S. Berman
Directed by Robert Z. Leonard
Screenplay by Marguerite Roberts and Sonya Levien
Based on a story by William Anthony McGuire
Photographed by Ray June
Musical numbers directed by Busby Berkeley
Musical score by Herbert Stothart
Musical direction by George Stoll
Running time: 134 minutes

Cast:
Gilbert Young . . . . James Stewart
Susan Gallagher . . . . Judy Garland
Sandra Kolter . . . . Hedy Lamarr
Sheila Regan . . . . Lana Turner
Frank Merton . . . . Tony Martin
Jerry Regan . . . . Jackie Cooper
Geoffrey Collis . . . . Ian Hunter
Pop Gallagher . . . . Charles Winninger
Noble Sage . . . . Edward Everett Horton
Franz Kolter . . . . Philip Dorn
John Slayton . . . . Paul Kelly
Patsy Dixon . . . . Eve Arden
Jimmy Walters . . . . Dan Dailey
Al Shean . . . . Himself
Mrs. Regan . . . . Fay Holden
Mischa . . . . Felix Bressart
Mrs. Frank Merton . . . . Rose Hobart

Ziegfeld Girl is an immense backstage musical into which MGM poured expensive talent by the ton. Designed to out-Ziegfeld Ziegfeld, the film fell just short of its lofty intentions. Producer Pandro S. Berman spared no effort in trying to make the picture one of Hollywood's greatest musicals. The star-studded cast is one of the biggest ever assembled, the music is plentiful and varied, Adrian's costumes and Cedric Gibbons's sets are sumptuous. Busby Berkeley again handled his massive movements with the practiced eye and technique that made him famous.

The film follows the paths of three girls who are glorified by Florenz Ziegfeld. Judy Garland, a vaudeville singer, is the daughter of old vaudevillian Charles Winninger, who plays the role of performer Pop Gallagher. Lana Turner is a department-store elevator operator loved by truck-driver James Stewart, and Hedy Lamarr is the wife of penniless violinist Philip Dorn. Judy becomes a Ziegfeld star with ease, but when Turner and Lamarr take to the glamorous life, they both have trouble with their men. The film's interest is in showing how Ziegfeld girls were chosen, where they came from, how they behaved, and what probably happened to some of them. It also shows how the producers of the Ziegfeld shows filled out their parades of gorgeous girls with specialty acts and comedy. The drama in *Ziegfeld Girl* centers on the reactions of the men in the lives of the girls. Charles Winninger is very appealing as an outdated performer trying to persuade his

daughter to follow in his footsteps, and yet it is due to his daughter that he is hired by Ziegfeld and reunited with his old partner Al Shean. Together they sing a celebrated Gallagher-and-Shean song and prove that the good things never really go out of fashion. Hedy Lamarr causes her husband anxiety when she dallies with singer Tony Martin, but eventually chooses her husband over her career, happily coinciding with his new opportunity as a concert violinist. The one real loser is James Stewart, who is jailed for bootlegging in an attempt to give Lana Turner the luxuries she wants. Lana's obsession with the theatre finally costs her her life.

Ziegfeld Girl contains a few old songs like "I'm Always Chasing Rainbows," "Mr. Gallagher and Mr. Shean," and a group of new ones, mostly by Roger Edens. Edens's "Ziegfeld Girls" is the setting for a lush stage deployment of fantastically lovely girls parading in traditional Ziegfeld manner—slowly and elegantly down staircases and around the stage. Walter Donaldson's song "You Never Looked So Beautiful" is included for obvious reasons.

Most of Busby Berkeley's activities in *Ziegfeld Girl* were concentrated on two lavish production numbers—an exotic tropical number, "Minnie From Trinidad," and the extravagant finale. "'Minnie' was a big calypso number with Tony Martin and Judy Garland both singing and dancing. I surrounded them with nearly two hundred boys and girls dressed in colorful native costumes, against a huge set of bamboo curtains and drapes. But the finale was the really big one here. Gus Kahn and Nacio Herb Brown wrote a marvelous song called 'You Stepped Out of a Dream,' and we saw this as a chance to present these wonderful girls as visions in dreams. Adrian outdid himself with his costumes for this number, as did Cedric Gibbons with his set—immense sixty-foot-high spiral staircases in gold and silver, adorned with massive cut-glass chandeliers and fantastic trimmings. Each girl emerged from a misty cloud effect, dripping with silver sequins. With all due respect to the master, Ziegfeld could never have done on a stage what we did in that finale."

The lovely and somnalescent Hedy Lamarr in her only musical appearance, here with co-stars Lana Turner and Judy Garland, assisted by assorted tulle- and feather-clad showgirls, in "You Stepped Out of a Dream."

S1165-21

"Minnie From Trinidad." The elaborate
calypso number with Judy Garland and
a chorus of more than two hundred.

LADY BE GOOD

An MGM Picture/1941
Produced by Arthur Freed
Directed by Norman Z. McLeod
Screenplay by Jack McGowan, Kay Van Riper, and
  John McClain
Photographed by George Folsey and Oliver T. Marsh
Songs: *Lady Be Good*
  Fascinatin' Rhythm
  Hang On to Me
    by George and Ira Gershwin

  The Last Time I Saw Paris
    by Oscar Hammerstein II and Jerome Kern

  You'll Never Know
  Your Words and My Music
    by Arthur Freed and Roger Edens

Musical numbers directed by Busby Berkeley
Musical direction by George Stoll
Running time: 110 minutes
Cast: Marilyn Marsh . . . . Eleanor Powell
  Dixie Donegan . . . . Ann Sothern
  Eddie Crane . . . . Robert Young
  Buddy Blue . . . . John Carroll
  Judge Murdock . . . . Lionel Barrymore
  Joe Willett . . . . Red Skelton
  Max Milton . . . . Reginald Owen
  Edna Wardley . . . . Rose Hobart
  Connie . . . . Connie Russell
  Virginia . . . . Virginia O'Brien
  Mr. Blanton . . . . Tom Conway
  Bill Pattison . . . . Dan Dailey

Lady Be Good bears little resemblance to the Gershwin stage musical of the same name, beyond retaining three of its songs. The film is notable for introducing a classic song, "The Last Time I Saw Paris," by Oscar Hammerstein II and Jerome Kern. It struck at a crucial time—soon after Paris had fallen to the Germans. That, coupled with the quality of the song itself, made it an immediate hit. At the following year's Academy Award presentations, "The Last Time I Saw Paris" won an Oscar as best film song of 1941.

Lady Be Good is about songwriting. The picture begins when an unsuccessful composer, Robert Young, meets waitress Ann Sothern in a restaurant. On a date he takes her to a music studio as his collaborator. Ann, an amateur lyricist, offers some of her work to the composer and it turns out to be just right. They form a songwriting team, become successful, and their friendship ripens into love and marriage. Once the toast of Tin Pan Alley, Young turns lazy and indolent. Ann leaves him, is granted a divorce by a kindly old judge, Lionel Barrymore, and then goes to live with her dancer friend, Eleanor Powell. A year goes by, when Ann gets a call from Young who is working on a song and needs her help. She goes to him; their love is rekindled. They marry, but the pattern repeats itself and once again Ann goes to Barrymore for a divorce, which is refused. Young, thinking the divorce has gone through, is remorseful and begs Ann to take him

Another white piano—this time, topped by Eleanor Powell. Robert Young, Ann Sothern, John Carroll, and Red Skelton also star.

back, promising to change his ways. She then reveals to him that they are still married.

The three Gershwin songs are used effectively, as is the great Hammerstein-Kern ballad and two new numbers by Arthur Freed and Roger Edens. Young comic Red Skelton, in one of his first screen appearances, scores as a daffy song-plugger, but it is the dancing of Eleanor Powell that truly highlights the picture. Of her three dances in *Lady Be Good*, the most spectacular is Berkeley's staging of "Fascinatin' Rhythm." A very intricate routine, it involved eight grand pianos and one hundred male dancers in white tie and tails, plus canes. Says Berkeley, "Eleanor was by far the finest female dancer we ever had in films, and a very hard-working perfectionist. This particular number was difficult for her because of the mechanics involved. She started the dance in front of a huge silver-beaded curtain, which circled to the left in a zig-zag course disclosing, on five-foot-high platforms, one grand piano after another. Eleanor followed and as the curtain circled each piano, a high-lift would move in, pick up the platform with the piano on it, and pull it back out of the way of the camera boom which was following Eleanor as she danced. All of this was filmed in one continuous shot until the last piano disappeared and the moving curtain revealed Eleanor in a huge circular set surrounded by the hundred boys, with a full orchestra in the background. Toward the end of this number, the boys would throw Eleanor like a pendulum down through the tunnel they formed, ending with a big close-up of her at the end of the shot. We rehearsed this trick over and over in order to get it right, and it was two in the morning by the time we finished. It was very hard on Eleanor physically; she was battered and bruised, but never complained. Not a whimper! She wouldn't give up until I had got what I wanted on film. After the preview of the picture she thanked me. I've known very few women that talented and that gracious."

Eleanor Powell and Berkeley rehearse for one of the
elaborate production numbers, "Fascinatin' Rhythm."

BABES ON BROADWAY

An MGM Picture/1941
Produced by Arthur Freed
Directed by Busby Berkeley
Screenplay by Fred Finklehoffe and Elaine Ryan
Photographed by Leslie White
Songs: How About You?
      Babes on Broadway
      Anything Can Happen in New York
      Chin Up, Cheerio, Carry On
      Hoe Down
      Bombshell from Brazil
      Franklin D. Roosevelt Jones
      Mama Yo Quiero

Musical direction by George Stoll
Running time: 118 minutes
Cast: Tommy Williams . . . . Mickey Rooney
      Penny Morris . . . . Judy Garland
      Barbara Jo . . . . Virginia Weidler
      Ray Lambert . . . . Ray McDonald
      Morton Hammond . . . . Richard Quine
      Jonesy . . . . Fay Bainter
      Mr. Stone . . . . Donald Meek
      Thornton Reed . . . . James Gleason

    Babes on Broadway, every bit as good as its predecessors, is the third of the Berkeley-Rooney-Garland trilogy. For pacing, vitality, and sheer good humor the three pictures form the best group of musicals made between the Astaire-Rogers films of the 1930's and the Kelly-Donen group of the early 50's. Few entertainers have ever matched the appeal and the ebullience of Judy Garland and Mickey Rooney at this stage in their lives. Backed in addition with

A publicity shot from the film.

the showmanship of producer Arthur Freed and an excellent selection of music, Busby Berkeley was able to direct a zestful piece of pure entertainment.

Once again the story deals with a group of youngsters, determined to succeed in show business. Mickey Rooney, Richard Quine, and Ray McDonald are three hoofers who call themselves The Three Balls of Fire. They get a call from their agent to appear at the office of grouchy Broadway producer James Gleason, whose warm-hearted secretary, Fay Bainter, tells the boys to turn up the next day for a private audition. Celebrating in a nearby drugstore, Rooney comes across Judy Garland, sitting alone and sobbing about her lack of luck as a singer. Rooney takes a shine to her and tries to cheer her up. Arriving at the theatre the next day for their audition, the boys find the place crawling with hopeful youngsters—news of the private audition having leaked out—and the irritated Gleason dismisses all of them, including Rooney and his chums. Rooney then decides to become a producer, but his spirits sag with the realization that he has no money. Hearing about a settlement home for poor children that is in need of funds, Rooney, Garland, and all their talented friends put together a musical. Just as the curtain is about to go up they are informed that the building has been condemned and the crowd cannot stay. The charitable audience takes this in good faith and files out without asking for their money back. Then producer Gleason turns up and, thanks to the badgering of Bainter, the kids perform their show just for him. Bowled over by their performance, Gleason signs them all to a contract for a Broadway musical.

Babes on Broadway is swept along by the cavorting of Rooney and Garland and an abundance of fine musical material. Ralph Freed and Burton Lane provided the memorable ballad "How About You" and the brisk title song. Composer Lane teamed with E. Y. Harburg for "Anything Can Happen in New York" and "Chin Up, Cheerio, Carry On," sung by a Garland surrounded by fifty British refugee kids—a timely patriotic touch and one which gave the picture added box-office strength in wartime Britain. Rooney, always keen on impersonation, vivaciously parodies Carmen Miranda as the Bombshell from Brazil. In a ghost sequence where they get on the cobwebbed stage of an old theatre in which many legendary actors have performed, Rooney imitates Walter Hampden as Cyrano de Bergerac and gives vigorous impressions of George M. Cohan and Sir Harry Lauder. Garland renders an impression of Sarah Bernhardt, struts like Fay Templeton, singing "Mary's a Grand Old Name," and Blanche Ring doing "Rings on Her Fingers."

Babes on Broadway includes Harold Rome's spirited song "Franklin D. Roosevelt Jones," marvelously sung by Judy Garland, and "Hoe Down" by Ralph Freed and Roger Edens, a 1941 jive number danced by a group of energetic youngsters. The finale is Busby Berkeley's version of a minstrel show. Long esteemed for his sense of the pictorial, Berkeley is now deft with hokum and humor and sensitive with tender-hearted sequences. Often viewed more as the Warner spectacles, rather than Berkeley work, these three musicals with Judy Garland and Mickey Rooney represent the peak of his peak career as a film-maker.

Mickey and Judy and the kind of good clean fun that makes Berkeley's films so joyful—here, the "Hoe Down" scene.

An unusual outdoor production number, singing the title song.

On stage with Mickey and Judy.

Mickey as the "Bombshell from Brazil."

Mickey with Carmen Miranda, the winner and still champion.

Judy Garland sings "Mary's a Grand Old Name" in a vaudeville setting.

Virginia Weidler in the Minstrel Show production sequence. Minstrel shows and Negro music are a popular motif in Berkeley's films.

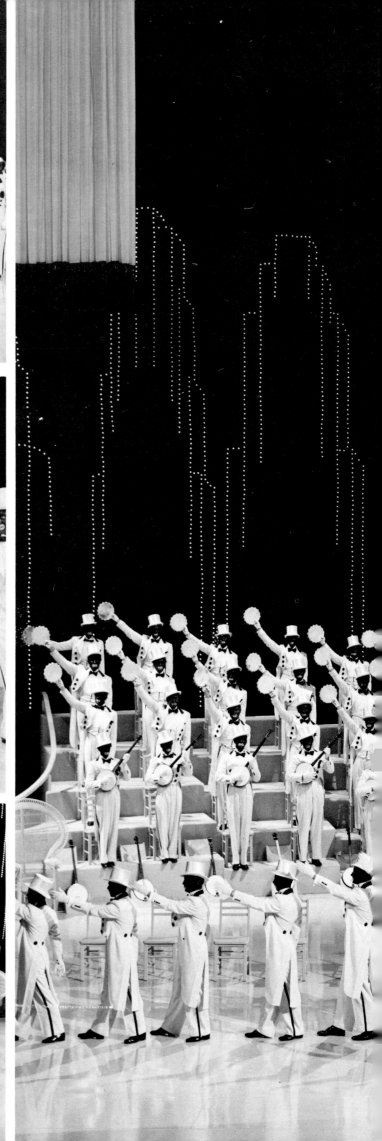

BORN TO SING

An MGM Picture/1942
Produced by Frederick Stephani
Directed by Edward Ludwig
Screenplay by Harry Clork and Franz G. Spencer
Photographed by Sidney Wagner
Finale created and directed by Busby Berkeley
Musical direction by Lennie Hayton and David Snell
Running time: 100 minutes

Cast: Patsy Eastman .... Virginia Weidler
Steve .... Ray McDonald
Grunt .... Rags Ragland
Joe .... Douglas McPhail
Pete Detroit .... Sheldon Leonard
Frank Eastman .... Henry O'Neill
Mike Conroy .... Larry Nunn
Snapper Collins .... Leo Gorcey
Maggie Cooper .... Beverly Hudson
Mozart Cooper .... Richard Hall
Quiz Kid .... Darla Hood
Dancer .... Maria Flynn
Ed Collers .... Joe Yule

"The Ballad for Americans," a musical sequence to inspire wartime America.

Born to Sing is one film where Berkeley was brought in to create a smash finale. In *Broadway Serenade* this turned out well because the Berkeley material was in character with the whole, but in *Born to Sing* the impressive staging of "The Ballad for Americans" comes at the end of a lackluster picture. Many critics of the time observed that it was like a short tacked on to the end of a feature.

Born to Sing like *Babes in Arms* has a group of youngsters doing a show but Virginia Weidler and Ray McDonald have difficulty measuring up to Rooney and Garland. Weidler plays a young girl whose father, a composer but an ex-convict, is being defrauded by an unscrupulous publisher. A trio of boys tries to help by making his music public in a show they whip together with neighborhood kids. Through the intervention of a friendly gangster and his hoodlums, the city's leading music and theatre critics are captured and forced to attend the opening night. All turns out well, with no explanation offered as to how the Berkeley finale is staged.

"The Ballad for Americans" was composed by folklorist Earl Robinson to a set of lyrics by poet John Latouche. A moving and rhapsodic statement of the American creed, it met with instant success at its premiere, sung by the great baritone Paul Robeson. MGM quickly purchased rights, and was then faced with the problem of how to use the piece. The studio turned to Busby Berkeley for a solution. "I've always enjoyed a challenge and this one was a pip. The lyrics were powerful and lengthy, telling as they do the object of America—the blending of all races and religions in democracy. The words had to be presented so that the audience could grasp them while at the same time I had to illustrate their meaning abstractly. I built a huge platform five feet high, covering one end of the sound stage, and in the center of this I had a revolving platform that telescoped upward to a height of forty feet and on which I could place people. I then had them build me odd shapes of blocks and pyramids about which I could move to get the different shots. The set was painted gray with nothing but a cyclorama of clouds for a background. Once the set was built I called rehearsals, and then with about two hundred people in front of me, I began to figure out my movements. This really took some thinking and a lot of time and work. Since the lyrics were about Americans of all kinds, I dressed my cast as people from every walk of life and had them parade over the corridors and byways of this huge set. The young baritone, Douglas McPhail, carried the main lyric and was gradually joined by sets of choruses, building to the finale. The result was beautiful, and the audiences used to cheer. Of course, it was wartime, and this kind of Americana had great impact. I felt, as did many, that the number should be released as a short. MGM didn't want to do this since they wanted to get their money out of the film as a whole, but they did send thirty prints of the sequence, on request, for the A.F.L. and the C.I.O., who distributed them to their branches. 'The Ballad for Americans' was, and is, a great piece of material and I was proud to be responsible for this presentation of it."

FOR ME AND MY GAL

An MGM Picture/1942
Produced by Arthur Freed
Directed by Busby Berkeley
Screenplay by Richard Sherman, Fred Finklehoffe,
   and Sid Silvers
Based on a story by Howard Emmett Rogers
Photographed by William Daniels
Musical adaptation by Roger Edens
Musical direction by George Stoll
Dance direction by Bobby Connolly
Running time: 100 minutes

Cast: Jo Hayden . . . . Judy Garland
        Harry Palmer . . . . Gene Kelly
        Red Metcalfe . . . . George Murphy
        Eve Minard . . . . Marta Eggert
        Sid Sims . . . . Ben Blue
        Lily Duncan . . . . Lucille Norman
        Danny Hayden . . . . Richard Quine
        Eddie Miller . . . . Keenan Wynn
        Bert Waring . . . . Horace McNally

Producer Arthur Freed recalls that at a meeting with his writers in preparing *For Me and My Gal*, a director was discussed and the decision quickly made. "Since this was a story about vaudeville and the struggles of a young couple to reach the top, we needed someone who knew the route, someone who knew about the hard work and heartaches that went with this way of life. The obvious choice was Buzz, who had lived this kind of story himself—it was his own background. Our only reservation in choosing him was that this was not simply a musical but an emotional story with some pathos and drama. It also contained a great deal of music, and we were a little afraid he might concentrate on that rather than the story. But he didn't. He came up with a very warm and human picture."

The story begins with a troupe of vaudevillians performing in a small town in Iowa. Among them are singer Judy Garland, who is sending her young brother through college, comic Ben Blue, dancer George Murphy, and singer-dancer Gene Kelly. Kelly convinces Garland that they would make a good team and that together they will soon appear at the Palace in New York. She agrees to join him, but two years pass and they are still in the small time. Kelly then meets singing star Marta Eggert and intrigues her with his breezy manner. Garland is jealous, but knowing how ambitious he is, she asks the star to help him. Kelly then realizes how much Garland means to him, and decides to stay with her rather than accept Eggert's offer. Eventually they reach the Palace but their joy is curtailed when Kelly receives his draft card. Determined not to give up his new success, he deliberately injures his hand in order to get a deferment. Garland learns of this at the same time she hears her brother has been killed in France, and she walks out on Kelly. He joins a YMCA entertainment unit and serves in France, proving himself a hero by an act of bravery. Looking for Garland he finds her entertaining soldiers in a canteen. Now reunited professionally and emotionally, they resume their career and after the Armistice proceed to the Palace as headliners.

A good many songs of the First World War are included in the troop entertainment sequences, and the vaudeville segments include such memorables as "Oh, You Beautiful Doll" and "After You're Gone." Kelly and Garland do a splendid dance routine to "Ballin' the Jack," and recorded the title song and "When You Wore a Tulip" as duets for Decca. As escapist entertainment for World War II audiences, *For Me and My Gal* succeeded completely.

A tender moment.

GIRL CRAZY

An MGM Picture/1943
Produced by Arthur Freed
Directed by Norman Taurog
Screenplay by Fred Finklehoffe
Based on the musical play by Guy Bolton and
 Jack McGowan
Photographed by William Daniels and Robert Planek
Songs by George and Ira Gershwin
Musical numbers directed by Busby Berkeley
Musical direction by George Stoll
Running time: 100 minutes
Cast: Danny Churchill, Jr. . . . . Mickey Rooney
  Ginger Gray . . . . Judy Garland
  Bud Livermore . . . . Gil Stratton
  Henry Lathrop . . . . Robert E. Strickland
  Rags . . . . Rags Ragland
  Specialty . . . . June Allyson
  Polly Williams . . . . Nancy Walker
  Phineas . . . . Guy Kibbee
  Marjorie Tait . . . . Frances Rafferty
  With Tommy Dorsey and His Orchestra

Busby Berkeley was to have directed *Girl Crazy* but he and producer Arthur Freed couldn't agree on a mutual concept, so Berkeley settled for directing only the song-and-dance portions. It was Mickey Rooney and Judy Garland's eighth film together, with Judy gradually overtaking Mickey in popularity. *Girl Crazy* is thoroughly entertaining and is performed with gusto by its young cast. It is also one of the few MGM musicals to use the score of the original stage show with few changes and no additions. Fred Finklehoffe's screenplay also sticks to the characters and story of Gershwin's Broadway musical of 1930.

Rich young playboy Mickey Rooney loves girls and they love him. This displeases his powerful publisher father who, to put an end to the boy's gallivanting, enrolls him in Custer College, Custerville, Arizona—a non-coeducational institution. The first person he meets at school is Judy Garland, granddaughter of the Dean. The affable Rooney settles into the school with ease and at once makes friends with his fellow students, but they become distressed at the news that the school is being closed because of insufficient enrollment. Rooney rallies his chums and their girl friends suggesting they stage a rodeo to win publicity and raise money for the school. Not only does Rooney secure a two months' extension on the school's closing from the state governor, but he meets the governor's beautiful daughter, Frances Rafferty, who invites him to her coming-out party. Rooney seizes the occasion to publicize his plans for the rodeo, telling each of a hundred debutantes that she is a cinch to be the rodeo queen. Judy's jealousy of Frances and the governor's objections to the rodeo being turned into a girlie show cause complications, but all ends well.

The Gershwin songs for *Girl Crazy* lost none of their sparkle and punch between 1930 and 1943, and it is doubtful if they have ever been given better performances than in this film. Judy Garland, in fine voice, sings "Embraceable You," "Bidin' My Time," and "But Not For Me," with young June Allyson and Rooney in "Treat Me Rough." Tommy Dorsey and His Orchestra appear in four of the numbers, including the rodeo finale built around "I've Got Rhythm." The hand of Berkeley is plainly apparent in the spectacular closing, which deploys one hundred dancing boys and girls and a complex of rodeo routines.

Mickey and Judy round up a rousing chorus of "I've Got Rhythm."

Carmen Miranda crowned by a tropical illusion after the
real thing was menaced by an inopportune swing of the
camera boom.

THE GANG'S
ALL HERE

THE GANG'S ALL HERE

A Twentieth Century—Fox Picture/1943
Produced by William LeBaron
Directed by Busby Berkeley
Screenplay by Walter Bullock
Based on a story by Nancy Wintner, George Root,
  and Tom Bridges
Photographed by Edward Cronjager
Songs: *A Journey to a Star*
  No Love, No Nothing
  The Lady in the Tutti-Frutti Hat
  The Polka Dot Polka
  Paducha
  Minnie's in the Money
  You Discover You're in New York
    by Leo Robin and Harry Warren

Musical direction by Alfred Newman
The Polka Dot Polka Ballet composed by
  David Raksin
Running time: 103 minutes
Cast: Eadie .... Alice Faye
  Rosita .... Carmen Miranda
  Phil Baker .... Himself
  Benny Goodman .... Himself
  Mr. Mason Sr. .... Eugene Pallette
  Mrs. Peyson Potter ... Charlotte Greenwood
  Peyson Potter .... Edward Everett Horton
  Tony DeMarco .... Himself
  Andy Mason .... James Ellison
  Vivian .... Sheila Ryan
  Sergeant Casey .... Dave Willock
  Specialty Dancer .... Miriam Lavelle

The Gang's All Here may be the film most characteristic of Berkeley's work, since it contains astounding effects and is a tribute to photographer Edward Cronjager. Producer William LeBaron obviously gave Berkeley full rein to come up with lavish, light movie entertainment perfectly suited to be wartime divertissement.

Alice Faye was at the height of her career as a star of movie musicals, but *The Gang's All Here* was her last. Married to Phil Harris and expecting a child at the time, she decided to retire from films after making one more picture, the dramatic *Fallen Angel*. Her place as the queen of Fox musicals was taken over by Betty Grable. *The Gang's All Here* also served as a starring vehicle for the flashy Brazilian bombshell, Carmen Miranda, who was never better displayed than in Berkeley's spectacular setting of "The Lady in the Tutti-Frutti Hat."

The plot is the tale of a showgirl, Alice Faye, in love with soldier James Ellison, who is engaged to his childhood sweetheart, Sheila Ryan. He marches off to war leaving two girls believing themselves engaged to him. When the girls meet, it becomes clear that the old sweetheart is more interested in a career than in marriage and the way is cleared for Faye and Ellison. The story is spiked with good comedy performances from Eugene Pallette as the

father of the soldier and Charlotte Greenwood and Edward Everett Horton as the parents of the girl who prefers her career. Phil Baker, then the star of radio's "Take It or Leave It," plays himself, and Benny Goodman and His Orchestra perform lustily in most of the numbers. Goodman even sings with Carmen Miranda in two songs.

Berkeley's composer cohort from the Warner days, Harry Warren, was teamed with him for the first time in five years—since *Garden of the Moon*. With lyricist Leo Robin, Warren provided two fine ballads for Alice Faye—"No Love, No Nothing" and "A Journey to a Star"—plus five brisk production pieces, the film's opener, "You Discover You're in New York," and two novelties—"Paducha" and "Minnie's in the Money." The truly spectacular efforts are lavished on "The Lady in the Tutti-Frutti Hat" and on the finale, "The Polka Dot Polka."

For "Tutti-Frutti," Berkeley built a set resembling a South Sea island, and sprinkled some sixty scantily clad, reclining native girls on the sand. In the trees there were real monkeys. Carmen Miranda appears in a gold cart drawn by two live gold-painted oxen, wearing a towering thirty-foot headdress of fruit and banana flowers. She plays a gigantic circular xylophone. At this time Berkeley was visited on the set by newspaperman Harold Heffernan, who filed the following account with the Detroit *News*:

Strange and devious are the ways of Hollywood directors. Cecil B. DeMille likes to bellow through a megaphone. Ernst Lubitsch is a floor-pacer and cigar-chewer. Gregory Ratoff insists on acting out every scene for his play-

A view of the finale through Berkeley's kaleidoscope-camera lens.

ers. And then there is Busby Berkeley, who has a passion for riding camera booms. Director Berkeley is never happier than when swooping down upon his players from the high cat-walks of a sound stage. We caught him in his favorite act on the set of *The Gang's All Here*, and here a catastrophe was averted only by the narrowest of margins. For this scene, Berkeley, strapped to a precarious seat beside the cameraman on the biggest boom in the studio, dives from unbelievable angles down upon harassed actors trying desperately to maintain character in the face of what looks to them like the attack of a P-40. The setting represents what is perhaps the biggest of all New York night clubs to be pictured on the screen, with Carmen Miranda up front singing. Despite the frantic gesticulations of Berkeley, the crane over-shoots its mark on the third take, coming to a dramatic halt a mere two inches above the cringing Miranda head. In passing, the runaway boom has completely dislodged the crazy Miranda headpiece. The flowers and fruit leaves that had been the creation's crowning glory are now strewn about the quivering Miranda feet. Stretching her full five feet, three inches of righteous anger, Carmen screams her indignation as Berkeley and the boom retreat to the farthest, highest corner of the stage. "That man 'ees crazee," Carmen announces. "What you theenk you are aneehow—a head hunter? Eef you wan' to keel me, why you don' use a gun?" From his position of safety, Berkeley cajoles and pleads. "Hokay," says Miranda; she'll risk her life just once more. "Thees time," she says soberly, "make weeth the careful! Knock one banana off my head and I will make of you the flat pancake!"

The finale of *The Gang's All Here* contains cinematic effects never before seen on the screen. Berkeley's mobile camera angles, the fluidity of movement, his dance compositions in the group numbers, his fondness for bizarre devices like water curtains tinted with rainbow lights, and his love affair with the kaleidoscope make this picture an amazing visual experience. The ending is film magic of vivid and fabulous abstractions. Recalls Berkeley, "I built a great kaleidoscope—two mirrors fifty feet high and fifteen feet wide which together formed a V design. In the center of this I had a revolving platform eighteen feet in diameter and as I took the camera up high between these two mirrors, the girls on the revolving platform below formed an endless design of symmetrical forms. In another shot, I dropped from above sixty neon lighted hoops which the girls caught and used in their dance maneuvers."

The finale, built around the song "The Polka Dot Polka," was orchestrated and developed into a ballet by composer David Raksin, giving Berkeley and his beautiful girls ample opportunity for involved movements. Whatever the merits of *The Gang's All Here* as a movie musical, it contains some of Berkeley's most imaginative work, proof that he refused to acknowledge any limitations in the medium of the screen.

"The Lady in the Tutti-Frutti Hat," resplendent with platform wedgies on a bed of bogus bananas. The cart is pulled by two live gold-painted oxen!

This sequence of giant dancing bananas was reportedly
banned in Brazil.

CINDERELLA JONES

A Warner Brothers Picture/1946
Produced by Alex Gottlieb
Directed by Busby Berkeley
Screenplay by Charles Hoffman
Based on a story by Philip Wylie
Photographed by Sol Polito
Songs: *If You're Waitin', I'm Waitin' Too*
       Cinderella Jones
        You Never Know Where You're Goin' 'Til
         You Get There
        When the One You Love Simply Won't Come
         Back
        by Sammy Cahn and Jule Styne

Background score by Frederick Hollander
Running time: 90 minutes

Cast: Judy Jones .... Joan Leslie
       Tommy Coles .... Robert Alda
       Camille .... Julie Bishop
       Bart Williams .... William Prince
       Gabriel Popik .... S. Z. Sakall
       Keating .... Edward Everett Horton
       Minland .... Charles Dingle
       Cora Elliott .... Ruth Donnelly
       Oliver S. Patch .... Elisha Cook, Jr.
       George .... Hobart Cavanaugh
       Mahoney .... Charles Arnt
       Krencher .... Chester Clute
       Riley .... Ed Gargan
       Marie .... Marianne O'Brien

Cinderella Jones, designed as a 1944 wartime musical comedy of modest proportions, might have succeeded if the original concept had been followed through. But Warner's held the picture on the shelf for a full two years, by which time many of the wartime references had lost their relevance and had to be deleted. The released product suffered from severe editing. The delay was due to Warner Brothers' decision to build Robert Alda's star status, waiting until he had exposure in their expensive production of *Rhapsody in Blue*, in which he played George Gershwin. The delay on *Cinderella Jones* was regrettable, because the Gershwin picture did not succeed as well as Warner's had anticipated and Alda never became a box-office attraction.

The title role of this musical farce is played by Joan Leslie. She appears as a pretty but not-too-bright young lady who is willed ten million dollars by her uncle under the proviso that she marry a man of unusual intelligence by a certain date. Her adventures include enrolling in a male college through a ruse, landing a job as a waitress, becoming a singer with a dance band, being jailed, almost drowning, and finally getting married on top of an army tank—one piece of wartime business Warner's could not excise from the picture. The cuts made in the film were damaging enough to confuse the story line and one reviewer suggested that customers should get a free second look at the picture in order to figure it out. While singing and dancing would have helped fill in the gaps, Joan Leslie breaks into song only sporadically. Robert Alda plays the band leader, who just happens to discover he has the required high IQ to qualify as the rich girl's husband.

The songs by veteran lyricist Sammy Cahn and young composer Jule Styne are typical of the time. Styne cut his teeth as a songwriter in Hollywood and in 1948 went to New York to become one of Broadway's best composers. For Busby Berkeley *Cinderella Jones* was an unfortunate picture, and the studio's decision to hold up its release coincided with a wave of bad luck in his personal life. Leaving the studio under a cloud of misunderstanding, Berkeley would now embark on several unhappy years and a huge hiatus in his film-making career.

From his start in Hollywood, Berkeley had

worked closely with Malcolm Beelby. Beginning with *Whoopee,* Beelby was assigned as Berkeley's rehearsal pianist and soon became his personal musical adviser. Berkeley would confer with Beelby on musical timings, estimating how many bars of music per camera sequence, with Beelby sometimes riding the camera boom and calling the cues. The two men are still close friends. Says Malcolm Beelby, "Buzz was a taskmaster, hard-driving and sometimes rough, but he inspired loyalty in the people who worked for him, and he excited their interest. He could be temperamental but behind the gruffness there was a kindness. For instance, in the Depression days he deliberately called for more crew than he actually needed—twenty men instead of perhaps six to move a camera crane. He hired as many girls as he could pack into a scene. He knew

they needed work. On the other hand, he was strangely hard on the producers and the heads of the studio, sometimes even humiliating them in front of the workers. This hurt his career. There were high-ranking film executives, who shall be nameless, who did nothing to help Buzz in his bad years. This is a hard business and Buzz had made things tough for himself but he didn't deserve the years of bad luck and being ignored by the studios."

Robert Alda plays a modern day Prince Charming to poor-little-rich-girl Joan Leslie, as S. Z. Sakall looks on.

TAKE ME OUT TO THE BALL GAME

An MGM Picture/1949
Produced by Arthur Freed
Directed by Busby Berkeley
Screenplay by Harry Tugend and George Wells
Based on an original story by Gene Kelly and
    Stanley Donen
Photographed by George Folsey
Songs: *The Right Girl for Me*
     It's Fate, Baby, It's Fate
     O'Brien to Ryan to Goldberg
     Strictly USA
     Yes, Indeed
     Take Me Out to the Ball Game
       by Betty Comden, Adolph Green, and
       Roger Edens

Musical direction by Adolph Deutsch
Running time: 94 minutes
Cast: Dennis Ryan .... Frank Sinatra
      K. C. Higgins .... Esther Williams
      Eddie O'Brien .... Gene Kelly
      Shirley Delwyn .... Betty Garrett
      Joe Logan .... Edward Arnold
      Nat Goldberg .... Jules Munshin
      Michael Gilhuly .... Richard Lane
      Slappy Burke .... Tom Dugan
      Zalinka .... Murray Alper
      Nick Donford .... William Graff

The film that brought Busby Berkeley back to the screen after a long and unfortunate absence was *Take Me Out to the Ball Game*. Says producer Arthur Freed, "Buzz wanted to get back to work and I wanted to help him, but it was a case of getting the right property for him. His was a very special talent and at this time in his life he couldn't afford to fail. Gene Kelly and Stanley Donen had written a story about a pair of baseball players who were also amateur vaudevillians in the era before the First World War, and this seemed to me just right for Buzz. He and Gene had gotten along well doing *For Me and My Gal* and this was more of the same kind of thing—old time show biz, lots of songs, dances, and fun. We talked it over and agreed on Buzz. And it worked out beautifully. Gene and Stanley did their own choreography, which took the strain off Buzz and allowed him to concentrate on the story and the comedy."

Asked to assess Busby Berkeley's contribution to the screen, Arthur Freed replies, "He was probably the most remarkable talent we had in the early days of movie musicals. He had an inborn camera sense, a fantastic eye. His creations are like dreams of the imagination. I consider him an instinctive surrealist, although I doubt if he himself has ever realized it. Like 'beauty is what beauty does,' Buzz just *is*."

Take Me Out to the Ball Game proved that Busby Berkeley had lost none of his directorial ability. The picture glides along with good humor and occasional excitement in telling of the adventures of baseball players Gene Kelly and Frank Sinatra, who also perform as song-and-dance men. Kelly is the slick one and Sinatra the shy type, with beauteous Esther Williams as the owner of their ball team. Esther falls in love with Kelly, who doesn't respond, and Sinatra yearns for Esther while being aggressively pursued by Betty Garrett. The plot detours to find racketeers trying to chisel in on the baseball business, with Edward Arnold as a wily gambler attempting to foil the efforts of Esther's team in the fight for the pennant. What happens in the story is less important than how it happens, and Berkeley bounces it along with verve.

Five new songs were written for *Take Me Out to the Ball Game* by musical comedy experts Betty Comden and Adolph Green. The vaudeville portions of the picture include "Take Me Out to the Ball Game" and some fine old songs like "The Hat My Father Wore on St. Patrick's Day," both of them danced with tremendous technique by Kelly. Sinatra croons to himself "The Right Girl for Me," and, with the effervescent Betty Garrett, sings and dances "It's Fate, Baby, It's Fate." Comedian Jules Munshin joins Kelly and Sinatra for a comic baseball number, "O'Brien to Ryan to Goldberg," and Kelly does more spirited hoofing and clowning with "Yes, Indeed" and "Strictly USA." The film concludes with a riotous baseball game, all amorous and sports equations solved.

Busby Berkeley was acclaimed for his comeback and for his handling of *Take Me Out to the Ball Game*, yet it was his last film as a director. In the remaining eight films of his career he would create and direct musical sequences only. Budget-minded producers were now extremely careful and undoubtedly cautious about hiring a man with a reputation for extravagance. One producer was heard to say, "Anyone who gave Berkeley an unlimited budget would be out of his mind."

In the December 1966 issue of *Cinema* magazine, Gene Kelly gave his opinion of Busby Berkeley: "Berkeley showed what could be done with a movie camera. A lot of that is made fun of nowadays; sometimes laughed at. But he was the guy who tore away the proscenium arch. He tore it down for movie musicals. Many get credit for that, but it was Berkeley who did it. And if anyone wants to learn what can be done with a movie camera, they should study every shot Busby Berkeley ever made. He did it all."

Esther Williams, who owns the baseball club, responds to cries of "kill the umpire."

Kelly clowns and The Chairman of the Board sings on.

Esther Williams, Frank Sinatra, Betty Garrett, Jules Munshin, and Gene Kelly tune-on the turn of the century. Can anyone identify the lady between Munshin and Kelly?

Take Me Out to the Ball Game/159

Song-and-dance-men Frank Sinatra and Gene Kelly in a moment of suspended animation.

TWO WEEKS WITH LOVE

An MGM Picture/1950
Produced by Jack Cummings
Directed by Roy Rowland
Screenplay by John Larkin and Dorothy Kingsley
Photographed by Alfred Gilks
Musical numbers staged by Busby Berkeley
Musical direction by George Stoll
Running time: 93 minutes

Cast:
Patti Robinson	Jane Powell
Demi Armendez	Ricardo Montalban
Horatio Robinson	Louis Calhern
Katherine Robinson	Ann Harding
Valerie Stresemann	Phyllis Kirk
Billy Finlay	Carleton Carpenter
Melba Robinson	Debbie Reynolds
Mr. Finlay	Clinton Sundberg
McCormick Robinson	Gary Gray
Ricky Robinson	Tommy Rettig
Eddie Gavin	Charles Smith

A charming period musical, *Two Weeks With Love* deftly employed a raft of old songs, ranging from semi-operatic material like "My Hero" and "Destiny" to ragtime pieces like "Row, Row, Row," "The Oceana Roll," and "Aba Daba Honeymoon," the film's hit song. Adding to the nostalgia were "By the Light of the Silvery Moon," "Down Among the Sheltering Palms," and "Beautiful Lady." Handsomely shot in Technicolor and delightfully staged, *Two Weeks With Love* is the story of a family in the early 1900's and their adventures, romantic and otherwise, at that perennial American paradise—the summer resort.

The father, Louis Calhern, a musician, and his wife, Ann Harding, take their brood of youngsters on their annual pilgrimage to a resort in the mountains. This summer, eldest daughter Jane Powell is reaching the age when the young female heart begins to flutter with romance. She falls in love with a handsome South American, Ricardo Montalban, whom she imagines to be her dream man. He is smitten with her but is noble enough not to take advantage of the girl's affections. Much is made of Jane's desperate urge to move from girlhood into young womanhood, the complicity of her brothers and sisters, and the concern of her parents. All through the trials and tribulations are a stream of musical numbers, sentimental and comedic; all delightfully staged by Busby Berkeley. The "Fourth of July" is given a humorous twist by having the elaborate fireworks display accidentally explode one night prematurely.

Jane Powell appeared at her winsome best in *Two Weeks With Love*, singing her pretty head off amid the frothy story line. The film is largely stolen, however, by the pleasing antics of Debbie Reynolds and Carleton Carpenter as a pair of teenage sweethearts; their performance of "Aba Daba Honeymoon" won enthusiastic approval. Debbie, then eighteen, had her fourth film part, and shortly afterward was given star billing in *Singing in the Rain*. The song "Aba Daba Honeymoon" was written as a vaudeville number in 1914 by Arthur Fields and Walter Donovan. It had been introduced at the Palace in New York by Ruth Roye, who made it one of her specialties. The song had been revised in 1930 for the Paul Whiteman film, *The King of Jazz*, but it was long gone and forgotten by the time it reappeared in *Two Weeks With Love*. The sound-track recording of the song sold over one million copies.

Debbie at eighteen, with Carleton Carpenter, steals the show with "Aba Daba Honeymoon."

CALL ME MISTER

A Twentieth Century–Fox Picture/1951
Produced by Fred Kohlmar
Directed by Lloyd Bacon
Screenplay by Albert E. Lewin and Burt Styler
Based on the musical play by Harold J. Rome and
   Arnold M. Auerbach
Photographed by Arthur E. Arling
Songs: *Call Me Mister*
     Going Home Train
     Military Life
       by Harold J. Rome

     I Just Can't Do Enough for You, Baby
     Japanese Girl Like American Boy
     Love is Back in Business
       by Mack Gordon and Sammy Fain

     Lament to the Pots and Pans
       by Jerry Seelen and Earl K. Brent

     I'm Gonna Love That Guy
       by Frances Ash

Dances directed by Busby Berkeley
Musical direction by Alfred Newman
Running time: 96 minutes
Cast:

Kay Hudson	Betty Grable
Shep Dooley	Dan Dailey
Stanley	Danny Thomas
Capt. Johnny Comstock	Dale Robertson
Billie Barton	Benay Venuta
Mess Sergeant	Richard Boone
The Kid	Jeffrey Hunter
Sergeant	Frank Fontaine
General Steele	Harry Von Zell
Jones	Dave Willock
Ackerman	Robert Ellis
Brown	Jerry Paris

Little beyond the title and story concept remained of Harold Rome's *Call Me Mister* when this film version was made almost six years after the Broadway musical. The film retained three of the original songs, added five new ones, and reunited Busby Berkeley with his old friend and director from the early Warner days, Lloyd Bacon, who showed he still knew how to mount a musical story and keep it moving entertainingly. This job was easier for Berkeley than most of his other musicals. He directed half a dozen dances along modest lines, but the finale, part of an army camp show, became ludicrously extravagant.

Dan Dailey, a GI at the end of the war, ready to be shipped home from Japan, discovers that his wife, from whom he has been separated, is serving with the Civilian Actresses Technician Service. He forges an assignment paper so he can help her stage a camp show and possibly win her back. The usual plot convolutions unravel to the desired end, with Grable and Dailey having plenty of opportunity to show off their dancing prowess.

Betty Grable, a Berkeley girl in *Whoopee*, had by now enjoyed a decade as a top Hollywood musical star, but before long her career would begin to decline along with the movie musical. In *Call Me Mister* she is in excellent form, particularly in "Japanese Girl Like American Boy," first singing with a chorus of Japanese girls and then in a sailor suit hoofing with a trio of male dancers, the Dunhills. She and Dailey sing and dance the film's title song and "I Just Can't Do Enough for You, Baby." Two numbers from the original Broadway show are "Military Life," a takeoff on Air Force heroes, and "Going Home Train," sung by Bobby Short, extolling the joys of soldiers returning to civilian life.

Danny Thomas appears in *Call Me Mister* with a comedy song written especially for him, "Lament to the Pots and Pans." He also takes part in the "Military Life" sequence as the guy who is "still a jerk" despite the uniform. Berkeley's finale, "Love is Back in Business," is entertaining but hopelessly out of keeping with the camp show setting.

Betty Grable, in "Japanese Girl Like American Boy," shows precisely why no one would ever call *her* Mister.

Grable and Dan Dailey lead the way, with Danny Thomas
and Benay Venuta behind.

With a spotlight on the stars, Berkeley gives us a glimpse from the heights of the camera boom.

TWO TICKETS TO BROADWAY

An RKO—Radio Picture/1951
Produced by Howard Hughes
Directed by James V. Kern
Screenplay by Sid Silvers and Hal Kanter
Based on a story by Sammy Cahn
Photographed by Edward Cronjager and Harry J. Wild
Songs: *Are You a Beautiful Dream?*
   The Closer You Are
   Baby, You'll Never Be Sorry
   Let the Worry Bird Worry for You
   Big Chief Hole-in-the-Ground
   Pelican Falls High
   It Began in Yucatan
    by Leo Robin and Jule Styne

Musical numbers created and directed by Busby Berkeley
Musical score by Walter Scharf
Running time: 106 minutes
Cast: Dan . . . . Tony Martin
   Nancy . . . . Janet Leigh
   Hannah . . . . Gloria DeHaven
   Lew Conway . . . . Eddie Bracken
   Joyce Campbell . . . . Ann Miller
   Bob . . . . Bob Crosby
   S. F. Rogers . . . . Barbara Lawrence
   Harry . . . . Joe Smith
   Leo . . . . Charles Dale
   Willard Glendon . . . . Taylor Holmes
   Sailor . . . . Buddy Baer

Two Tickets to Broadway is replete with a large selection of songs, dances, specialties, skits, acrobatics, and even a little grand opera.

The film gave Tony Martin his best screen opportunity in years. In addition to the new songs, Martin sings a few of his standards: "There's No Tomorrow," "Manhattan," and the Prologue from "Pagliacci." *Two Tickets to Broadway*, despite its title, is actually about television and was one of Hollywood's first films to editorialize the new medium.

Janet Leigh appears as the pert young lady with theatrical ambition, who boards a bus in Pelican Falls, Vermont, to the accompaniment of cheers and songs from her school chums. This fanciful picture of life in a small town is reminiscent of the Warner musicals of the 30's. In New York Janet soon learns about the tough life of the entertainment business when she meets three girls who have been stranded by a flop production. Through them she finds lodging in a friendly girls' boarding house. The quartet—Janet, Ann Miller, Gloria DeHaven, and Barbara Lawrence—comes under the influence of agent Eddie Bracken, who rehearses them in an act hoping to get them on the Bob Crosby TV Show. Trials and tribulations precede their appearance, during the course of which Janet meets and falls for unemployed singer Tony Martin. Disgusted by the frustrations of show business and what she imagines to be double-dealing by Martin, she is about to board the bus back to Pelican Falls when word arrives that the girls are booked for the Crosby Show. The act is a smash hit, as is Martin's own show, and the pair reunite, explaining the misunderstandings.

Two Tickets to Broadway gave Busby Berkeley several production numbers to stage as features for television variety shows, in addition to the opening send-off in Pelican Falls. The seven new songs written by Leo Robin and Jule Styne served their purpose. The vivacious dancing of Ann Miller scored in her routine, "Let the Worry Bird Worry for You." Millionaire Howard Hughes was credited with being the film's producer but the real work at the RKO studio was done by Jerry Wald. Berkeley remembers that he was called in to start staging his musical numbers before the script was completed—"Always a bad sign."

Playing the classic ingenue, tender, young Janet Leigh is a duo with Tony Martin, while Gloria de Haven looks on enviously.

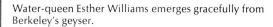

Esther Williams is at her best in *Million Dollar Mermaid* as Annette Kellerman, the Australian swimming champion of the 1920's who made an even bigger splash for herself when she crossed over into show business. The highlight of her career was her aquatic performance at the New York Hippodrome, and to recreate the event, Busby Berkeley used two sets—one with water fountains and the other with colored smoke streams.

The story begins in Australia with Annette Kellerman, a crippled child who regains her health by swimming. She becomes the amateur champion of New South Wales. When her musician father, Walter Pidgeon, loses his business they decide to head for England where she wins attention through swimming and comes into contact with American promoter Victor Mature. He induces her to swim twenty-six miles down the Thames as a publicity stunt, then persuades her to go to New York, where he is sure to get her a booking at the New York Hippodrome. They are unsuccessful, and go to Boston, where a sensation is created over her arrest for indecent exposure while wearing a one-piece bathing suit at a time when women wore only voluminous swimsuits. Her subsequent trial results in national publicity and acts as a springboard to fame. Ultimately, the

MILLION DOLLAR MERMAID

An MGM Picture/1952
Produced by Arthur Hornblow, Jr.
Directed by Mervyn LeRoy
Screenplay by Everett Freeman
Photographed by George J. Folsey
Two sequences directed by Busby Berkeley
Musical direction by Adolph Deutsch
Running time: 115 minutes
Cast: Annette Kellerman . . . . Esther Williams
James Sullivan . . . . Victor Mature
Frederick Kellerman . . . . Walter Pidgeon
Alfred Harper . . . . David Brian
Annette (10 years) . . . . Donna Corcoran
Doc Cronnol . . . . Jesse White
Pavlova . . . . Maria Tallchief
Aldrich . . . . Howard Freeman
Policeman . . . . Charles Watts
Garvey . . . . Wilton Graff
Prosecutor . . . . Frank Ferguson
Judge . . . . James Bell
Conductor . . . . James Flavin
Director . . . . Willis Bouchey

A publicity still shows Esther recreating Annette Kellerman's most spectacular number—a fantastic frolic of fire and water, complete with Fourth of July sparklers.

sensational swimmer is booked into the New York Hippodrome, where she is extremely well received. A romantic triangle develops with Hippodrome manager David Brian and Mature, who is too proud to admit he loves her. Mature stalks off, but returns when he has found fame for himself as the discoverer of superdog Rin Tin Tin, ultimately winning back his swimmer.

The role of Annette Kellerman was tailor-made for Esther Williams who looks marvelous in her swimming apparel and whose skill equaled Miss Kellerman's. The underwater choreography was directed by Audrene Brier, and above-water antics were arranged by Berkeley.

Known as The Million Dollar Dance Director, Berkeley provides more evidence in this film of how and why he held the title. For the fountain number, Esther Williams does a specialty act in a huge water tank (supposedly on the stage of the New York Hippodrome), under a canopy of four hundred streams of water which shoot up thirty feet to form a massive waterfall. Esther rises from the center of the pool on top of a geyser and from there performs a forty-foot swan dive. Technicolor enhances the effect with multi-hued waters.

The smoke number is even more impressive.

Berkeley obviously enjoys having created this spectacle. "I used one hundred boy and girl swimmers and for the background I had nothing but red and yellow smoke streams shooting up fifty feet. The effect was made by four hundred electrically controlled smoke pots. On each side of the pool, I had forty-foot-high ramps, from which the swimmers slid down at a terrific pace, standing up and carrying yellow lighted torches as they entered the water. I also had twelve long swings that swung down from high in the air through the smoke, and from which twelve girls and twelve boys simultaneously dived into the water. Esther was also the center of attention in this number. I dropped her from fifty feet into the mass of swimmers below, which exploded into a ferris-wheel effect on the water. Then they all submerged, and gradually out of the water came Esther on a platform surrounded by beautiful girls. The closing effect was an array of five hundred lighted sparklers coming out of the water and forming a background around the whole group."

Million Dollar Mermaid was deservedly well received by the public. The reviews never failed to credit the fountain and smoke numbers as magnificent sequences, with Berkeley hailed as still the master of the spectacular.

"If you've got it, flaunt it," and Esther's got it—her chain-mail bathing suit is composed of 50,000 gold flakes.

From formation dancing to formation swimming—a human waterflower.

Swimmers swing into action.

SMALL TOWN GIRL

An MGM Picture/1953
Produced by Joe Pasternak
Directed by Leslie Kardos
Screenplay by Dorothy Cooper and Dorothy
   Kingsley
Photographed by Joseph Ruttenberg
Songs: *My Flaming Heart*
     Small Towns Are Smile Towns
     My Gaucho
     The Lullaby of the Lord
     I've Gotta Hear That Beat
     Take Me to Broadway
     Fine, Fine, Fine
     The Fellow I'd Follow
     by Leo Robin and Nicholas Brodszky

Musical numbers staged by Busby Berkeley
Musical direction by André Previn
Running time: 95 minutes
Cast: Cindy Kimbell . . . . Jane Powell
     Rick Belrow Livingstone . . . . . Farley Granger
     Lisa Bellmount . . . . Ann Miller
     Eric Schlemmer . . . . S. Z. Sakall
     Judge Gordon Kimbell . . . . Robert Keith
     Ludwig Schlemmer . . . . Bobby Van
     Mrs. Livingston . . . . Billie Burke
     Mrs. Gordon Kimbell . . . . Fay Wray
     Nat King Cole . . . . Himself
     Mac . . . . Dean Miller
     Ted . . . . William Campbell
     Hemingway . . . . Philip Tonge
     Jim . . . . Jonathan Cott
     Dennis . . . . Bobby Hyatt

Small Town Girl is a Joe Pasternak production, a slick, glossy, pleasing picture made by a man who seldom failed in his attempts to reach a large audience. The film is gay and sprightly, loaded with the singing of Jane Powell and the dancing of Ann Miller. The story is mainly a peg for the eight musical numbers.

The film makes quite a case for the virtues of life in a small town. Farley Granger, a spoiled millionaire playboy, is given a thirty-day sentence by Judge Robert Keith for speeding at eighty-five miles per hour through the streets of Duck Creek. Granger is engaged to Broadway star Ann Miller, but upon meeting the judge's daughter, Jane Powell, he becomes enamoured—emotionally torn between Duck Creek and New York—with no doubt in anyone's mind as to the outcome of the predicament.

In the sub-plot, young Bobby Van is the small-town boy who wants to leave his life as a clerk in the emporium owned by his father, S. Z. Sakall, to try for a career as a song-and-dance man in the theatre. He makes his ambitions plain in "Take Me to Broadway." Nat King Cole, appearing as himself, sings the film's primary ballad, "My Flaming Heart," but the major song burden falls on petite soprano Jane Powell. Jane lays it on the line for Duck Creek with "Small Towns are Smile Towns," and for the kind of man she admires with "The Fellow I'd Follow." She and Bobby Van with eight pretty young girls sing "Fine, Fine, Fine."

Ann Miller is particularly effective in *Small Town Girl*, proving again that she was among the very best dancers in Hollywood. She and a male octet sing and dance "My Gaucho," but it was "I've Gotta Hear That Beat" that Berkeley recalls as one of his most difficult assignments. "Leo Robin had to think of a lyric for Ann Miller and couldn't. He asked me if I had any ideas, and all I could point out was that Ann's forte was tap-dancing, and maybe he could build something around that. Several days later he handed me a lyric titled 'I've Gotta Hear That Beat.' I looked at it—blankly. I needed something that would in turn give me an idea, and this suggested nothing very much. I complained to Leo and he shrugged, 'Sorry, Buzz, you'll have to take it from there.' The picture was already in production and I was rehearsing Bobby Van's number. Then Pasternak came up and asked me what I wanted as a set for the Ann Miller number. I told him I hadn't even had a chance to think about it, to which he replied, 'Well, hurry up, we haven't got much time.' The old familiar situation. The next day while I was shooting Bobby's number I got an idea for Ann. I asked them to build me a stage five feet high that would cover one end of a studio floor, with a small platform in the rear and steps coming down either side. My idea was to place eighty-six musicians under this stage and drill holes for their arms. From the top you would then see all these arms with musical instruments sticking up through the floor as Ann danced around them. As she sang 'I've Gotta Hear That Beat,' she would get it from the various disembodied instruments. I worked late into the night on my graph-drawings, figuring out the positions of the instruments so I could tell the carpenters where to drill the holes, and the sequence of the camera tracking. I explained this to Pasternak, who went pale and said, 'I hope to hell you know what you're doing because I don't.' Word spread around the studio that I'd probably flipped out this time, but I'd heard that before. We started filming it the next day and it worked like a charm."

Ann Miller tapping to "My Gaucho."

Strictly undercover, Berkeley pushes his way through seemingly headless musicians who provide arms and instruments.

174/Small Town Girl

Ann Miller sings "I've Gotta Hear That Beat."

Small Town Girl/175

boss, Van Johnson, that she works for him as the star of his aquatic show and doubles as his secretary, all for seventy-five dollars a week and without recognition from him either for her efforts or affection. Showing no interest in the advances made by swimming instructor John Bromfield or by New York singer Tony Martin, she allows them to court her only as a means of making Johnson jealous. Finally seeing the light, he puts up a fight to win the girl.

The music in *Easy to Love* rests almost entirely on Tony Martin, whose voice was then in its prime. He sings the old Cole Porter song that gives the picture its title, and "Coquette," one of Johnny Green's first hit songs. Of the three new songs written for the film, Martin sings "That's What a Rainy Day Is For" with a group of sixteen elderly ladies. "Look Out! I'm Romantic" and "Didja Ever" are sung by Martin in a New York nightclub.

Easy to Love involves three aquatic numbers directed by Busby Berkeley. In one, Esther Williams, made up as a clown, cavorts around a swimming pool with a large chimpanzee, much to the delight of the children who are watching. In another, she is teamed with John Bromfield, romantically swimming in a moonlit cove blanketed by floating white gardenias. While they swim, violinists, each attached to a cypress tree by a small platform at water-level, serenade.

The finale, photographed mainly from a helicopter hovering over Florida's Lake Eloise, gave Berkeley an exciting challenge. "This was the kind of thing I loved. I had Esther and eighty boy and girl skiers whizzing along on skis carrying big flags. I mapped out an intricate pattern of movements for them through the cypress trees and around huge geysers that shot sixty-foot sprays into the air. I had twelve boy skiers going over twelve-foot-high jumps simultaneously. In one part of the routine I used a hundred girls in a huge swimming pool that I had had built in the shape of the state of Florida. I used a helicopter in another part of this sequence, with Esther standing on a trapeze while hanging from the plane, then diving from a height of eighty feet into a V-shaped formation of skiers traveling at thirty-five miles per hour across the lake. She then comes up on skis for a furious ride that takes her looping over several ramps; finally hurtling over the heads of the bandsmen, who are merrily playing away, and comes right up to the camera. I wanted to create the effect that she might land right in the audience. I might have been able to do that had we had 3-D."

Berkeley's aquatic routines in *Easy to Love* rank among the most outstanding pieces of action ever filmed. Ernie Shier, writing in the New York *Journal-American*, summed up the feelings of many:

> I'd say this was Busby Berkeley's crowning achievement. He's the man who for years has been throwing staggering musical numbers, filled with beautiful girls, at audiences. The topper is the big finale when Esther takes to water skis and leads a whole danged parade of boys and girls, in yellow and black costumes, through a triumphant processional that is showier than the recent Coronation and paced faster than a Keystone Cops comedy.

The Baroque apotheosis of the water nymph—Esther Williams's finale.

ROSE MARIE

An MGM Picture/1954
Produced and directed by Mervyn LeRoy
Screenplay by Ronald Miller and George Froeschel
Based on the operetta by Otto Harbach and Oscar
   Hammerstein II
Photographed by Paul Vogel
Songs: *Rose Marie*
   The Indian Love Call
   The Mounties
   Totem Tom Tom
      by Otto Harbach, Oscar Hammerstein II,
      and Rudolf Friml

   The Right Place for a Girl
   Free to Be Free
   Love and Kisses
   I Have Love
      by Paul Francis Webster and Rudolf Friml

   The Mountie Who Never Got His Man
      by Herbert Baker and George Stoll
Musical numbers staged by Busby Berkeley
Musical direction by George Stoll
Running time: 103 minutes
Cast: Rose Marie Lemaître . . . . Ann Blyth
   Mike Malone . . . . Howard Keel
   James Severn Duval . . . . Fernando Lamas
   Barney McCorkle . . . . Bert Lahr
   Lady Jane Dunstock . . . . Marjorie Main
   Wanda . . . . Joan Taylor
   Inspector Appleby . . . . Ray Collins
   Black Eagle . . . . Chief Yowlachie

This third filming of the Rudolf Friml operetta is distinguished as the first musical made in Cinemascope, employing sequences filmed in color in the Canadian Rockies and the California Sierras. Busby Berkeley's efforts in this edition of *Rose Marie* were mainly concerned with the staging of a comic routine for Bert Lahr and an Indian ceremonial dance of epic proportions.

Rose Marie has been presented in several widely different fashions. In the 1924 Broadway original, the lady of the title was a cute little bushmaiden in love with a brave young fur-trapper. In order to save his life she was forced to accept the attentions of a villain, who is later nabbed by a Mountie. MGM bought the rights to the musical, and in their first version filmed in 1928 with Joan Crawford playing the lead, Rose Marie nursed a dying husband between amorous scenes with both the trapper and the Mountie. The 1928 version was silent except for a printed musical score for piano, organ, or full orchestra that accompanied each copy of the picture. In the larger presentation houses, an off-stage singer accompanied the "Indian Love Call" sequence. MGM remade the story in 1936 as one of the most successful of the Jeanette MacDonald–Nelson Eddy vehicles, but this time the leading lady was an opera star, the trapper became her delinquent brother, and the Mountie moved into co-star status as a singing lover. In Mervyn LeRoy's 1954 setting, Rose Marie became a pretty little waif of the forest who fell in love with a handsome trapper of doubtful character, with the Mountie in brotherly surveillance.

Many of the original characters were dropped in this version and a few new ones were added. A new plot twist has the beautiful daughter (Joan Taylor) of an Indian Chief (played by a genuine Chief named Yowlachie) madly and vainly in love with the trapper. Her father whips her for running after a white man, and she kills him with the trapper's knife, implicating him in the crime. The trapper is arrested and is on the way to the gallows when the Mountie forces the truth from the Indian girl in order to save the trapper's life. While all this has been going on, Rose Marie has been brought in from the bush and sent by soft-hearted Mountie inspector Ray Collins to receive a social education from his cousin, Marjorie Main. Miss Main, the gruff operator of a saloon-hotel, has a soft heart, sought by Bert Lahr, a blundering, buffoon-like Mountie whose image may possibly have offended the Canadians, but amused his many fans.

Four of the original songs were used in this filming of *Rose Marie*: the title song, "The Mounties," "The Indian Love Call," and "Totem Tom Tom." Rudolf Friml, then seventy-two, was hired to provide four new songs in collaboration with lyricist Paul Francis Webster: "The Right Place for a Girl," with Keel lecturing the wild Rose Marie; "Free to Be Free," in which Rose Marie states her case; "I Have Love," with Blyth and Lamas plighting their troth; and "Love and Kisses," a rollicking anti-romance duet sung by Bert Lahr and Marjorie Main. With an excellent piece of material written for him by George Stoll and Herbert Baker—"The Mountie Who Never Got His Man"—Lahr laments his long career as an unsuccessful Mountie, acting out his misadventures to a gathering of guests and workers in the hotel lounge.

The choreographic spectacle in *Rose Marie* is Berkeley's "Totem Tom Tom," an elaborate Indian ceremonial dance featuring Joan Taylor and some hundred Indian braves. "We rehearsed this number for a month and it ended up costing two hundred thousand dollars. We used Stage 15 at MGM, then the largest sound stage in the world, and turned it into a mountain stronghold. We tried to make the number as dramatic and frenzied as possible, and as the climax I had one of the Indians grab Joan Taylor, lift her over his head, and throw her from a cliff fifty feet high into the outstretched arms of the Indians below, who then bound her to a great totem pole. It was an exciting routine to stage, and people seemed to be very impressed with it."

An Indian warrior selects his bride, Hollywood, 1954.

"Over and Over Again" is sung by Doris who then does her act on the revolving ladder.

The story of *Jumbo* is as old as the circus. Doris Day is the daughter of circus-owner Jimmy Durante, a charming old boy given to gambling, at which he seldom wins. His one major asset is a magnificent elephant, Jumbo. Rival circus owner Dean Jagger, scheming to bankrupt Durante and gain ownership of the beast, sends his handsome son, Stephen Boyd, into the Durante camp as an undercover agent. Boyd, hired as a trapeze artist by Durante, goes about his plans to sabotage the circus. But Boyd falls in love with the lovely Doris and gradually grows ashamed of what he is doing to the point of turning against his father and helping the Durante outfit to succeed rather than fail.

Jimmy Durante starred in the original *Jumbo*, and it was only poetic justice that he should star in the film which contained what is possibly his most famous bit of business. Having lost his beloved pachyderm to his rival, Durante sneaks out one night to steal her back. Surreptitiously leading the gigantic animal away, Durante is halted by the booming voice of a sheriff: "Where are you going with that elephant?" His face a mask of indignation and innocence, Durante looks around to reply, "What elephant?"

In its musical score *Jumbo* retained the original Rodgers and Hart songs—"The Circus on Parade," "Over and Over Again," "The Most Beautiful Girl in the World," "My Romance," and "Little Girl Blue." It borrowed two other Rodgers and Hart classics—"Why Can't I?" from *Spring Is Here* (1929) and "This Can't Be Love" from *The Boys from Syracuse* (1938). For the film's finale Roger Edens wrote "Sawdust, Spangles and Dreams," which reprised some Rodgers and Hart material.

As the film's second unit director, Busby Berkeley was responsible for the opening sequence in which the Durante circus arrives in town and parades in all its glory through the turn-of-the-century streets. He also shines in the "Over and Over Again" sequence in which Doris Day and a group of skillful trapeze artists spin and revolve in the air under the Big Top. The pageantry of the parade and the dazzle of the aerial ballet are unmistakably Berkeley. Various other circus acts were under his direction.

Doris Day trained for the acrobatics in *Jumbo*. Recalls Berkeley, "For Doris's equestrienne act I had them rig a big turntable high up over the center ring. On one side I hung a trapeze for Doris, and on the other side I had a camera platform. While riding, Doris did tricks on the horse's back and then stood up and grabbed the trapeze, which took her up high into the air. She swung in a circle over the ring, then came down and landed on the back of the horse. It was a thrilling number to film, as well as to watch, and I think she did it beautifully."

High-flying Stephen Boyd rescues marooned aerialist Doris, who did her own trapeze stunts.

Actress Ruby Keeler is bussed by Busby Berkeley after the Broadway opening of *No, No, Nanette*, January 19, 1971.

NO, NO, NANETTE

The retrospective showing of Busby Berkeley's films in the late 1960's—the great interest in seeing them and their widespread appreciation—was part of a rising tide of nostalgia. The cacophony of modern living, the harshness and the cynicism of contemporary means and methods, had left an increasing number of people with the desire to look to past eras. Sentimental yearnings for days gone by always have been stock-in-trade in the entertainment business, and by 1970 this was becoming a general trend for movie and theatregoers as well.

The revival of Vincent Youmans's 1925 musical comedy, No, No, Nanette, on Broadway in January 1971 was the apotheosis of this trend. The backers and producers were confident of success—confident enough to invest more than half a million dollars— but even they were astounded by the public reaction to this dated vehicle of the Roaring '20's. No, No, Nanette had no more relevance to 1971 than a flapper to a hippie, yet it was staged with such verve and vitality that it became an immediate smash. Within one week of the opening it was the best Broadway bet in New York.

Busby Berkeley had been approached early in 1970 with the possibility of staging the Youmans musical. The backers knew their man. Berkeley had worked with Youmans in Broadway theatres all through the 1920's. Anyone who had ever seen a Berkeley film knew that his touch was unique and that his sensibilities were needed to successfully put over an old musical on the new Broadway. The question was whether or not at the age of seventy-five he was up to the job. It only took one interview to learn that the Berkeley mind was as active as ever and that the Grand Old Man of movie musicals was ready, willing, and able.

Berkeley was hired as the supervising producer of No, No, Nanette to advise the producer, the director, designers, and the choreographer. In one area—picking the chorus girls—he was supreme commander, auditioning 350 young lovelies in order to assemble the chorus line of 22.

No, No, Nanette opened in New York at the 46th Street Theatre on January 19, 1971, and those who were there are not likely to ever forget it. The atmosphere was electric with warmth and appreciation. Each song and dance brought waves of applause, and when Ruby Keeler started tap-dancing to "I Want to Be Happy," the audience cheered and screamed. Ruby, retired for thirty years, had only to walk onto the stage to learn how well she had been remembered. The name Ruby Keeler symbolized one of filmland's favorite decades—the fabulous 1930's. At the end of the evening, the company took bow after bow. Then comedienne Patsy Kelly walked offstage, returning hand-in-hand with a white-haired gentleman. The audience broke apart, everyone coming to his feet, yelling "Busby Berkeley! Busby Berkeley!" over and over again.

The critics surrendered. Charles Mac Harry of the New York Daily News headed his column "Love Letter" and wrote:

> Dear Busby Berkeley, Ruby Keeler, Jack Gilford, Patsy Kelly, Helen Gallagher, Bobby Van, the two pianos, the orchestra, etc.— whoever you are and everyone connected with Broadway's revival of 1925's No, No, Nanette. You, collectively, are darlings. I have never attended an opening night that generated more enthusiasm, and may I say I whooped, applauded and otherwise cheered with all the others? I could not have been happier if I had been a backer.

Index